Richard Howitt

Wasps Honey

Poetic Gold and Gems of Poetic Thought

Richard Howitt

Wasps Honey
Poetic Gold and Gems of Poetic Thought

ISBN/EAN: 9783337777937

Printed in Europe, USA, Canada, Australia, Japan

Cover: Foto ©Thomas Meinert / pixelio.de

More available books at **www.hansebooks.com**

OR,

POETIC GOLD

AND

GEMS OF POETIC THOUGHT.

BY

RICHARD HOWITT.

It may be a medicine, may also be wine,
Of body of flavour delicious, divine:
Yet ere it can reach the unsatisfied soul,
Some traitor may poison, or dash down the bowl.

LONDON:
J. M. DARTON AND CO., PUBLISHERS,
42, PATERNOSTER ROW.
SOLD BY ALL BOOKSELLERS.
1868.

LITERARY NOTICES.

" Nature has been bountiful to you."—*Alfred Tennyson.*

" I think my own verses honoured by being interwoven with yours, in a poem treated with such depth of feeling."—*Words-worth.*

" I feel respect for your talents, and esteem for the manner in which you employ them. You have earned a name beyond your family one by good deeds in song."—*James Montgomery.*

" The story of 'The Gipsy King' is full of genuine pictures of Nature, animate and inanimate."—*Leigh Hunt.*

" This writer aims to make poetry not the mere slave of pride or pleasure, but a minister of good. With Wordsworth's bald-ness, abruptness, and sometimes even with his affected sim-plicity, he has much of his sustained elevation of mind, and of his inspiring philosophy. He loves nature, not merely because nature is beautiful, but because its contemplation is calculated to fill the mind with thoughts profound, and to bring man into solemn communion with the mysterious Power of the universe."—*London Saturday Journal,* 1840.

" A writer of true poetical feeling, and considerable poetical power."—*Blackwood's Magazine.*

" He has a fine taste for Nature in all her simplicity : a keen perception of the beauties of the natural world. He writes affectionately, and unaffectedly. We recommend his book to the million of readers who study nature in books, if not in the fields. He is healthfully English in his compositions."—*Athenæum,* 1810.

PREFACE.

POETS have delighted themselves with the figurative idea that they were bees, and their poetry honey. Campbell, Moore, and Rogers entertained that fabulous notion, but merry Mr. Perry, the critic, laughed at them, and stung them with the rumour that they were *wasps*. And waspish enough some poets have been. Even amiable Cowper made use of the " thorns and briars of reproof." And

> " Pope entertained the whim
> Who feared not God should be afraid of him."

Also Byron might have applied to himself his own couplet,

> " There was a laughing devil in his sneer,
> That raised emotions both of rage and fear."

Sneers that woke duels. I am no satirist; I never could read the Dunciad. Byron's satirical honey was that of asps and scorpions; the satire of Burns played round him like sportive lightning, blasting and scorching. I cannot think that satire ever did any good; but that truthful pictures of human character do. Satire seems to me useless, for these reasons :— fear stupefies, hate irritates and hardens; but love melts and wins. Love is the only universal civilizer.

Unimaginative people may aver that there is no such thing as wasps' honey ; but poets, who live in two worlds, the actual and the ideal, know better. It is their vocation

    " To body forth the forms of things unknown,"

and

                    " to make
The thing that is not, as the thing that is."

Therefore, good reader, have full faith in the two great poets whom I have quoted, that

    " Such might hath strong imagination."

Sharp, racy, and pungent, must be the honey of gorse, brambles, and also of that rough, burly, Scottish national symbol, the thistle. This last desperate weed is also the symbol of a sharp sincerity, and of the poetry of truth. If not the John Milton, it is the John Knox of plants. The Bee thinks

    " That nothing of itself will come,
      But it must still be seeking."

Yes, the Bee is *a slave;* but the wasp

> " Both man and boy
> Has been an idler in the land,
> Contented if he might enjoy
> The things which others understand."

That is it—bees *understand* honey, but wasps *enjoy* it. Poets and bees *were* martyrs—but now in this improved age—thanks to the critics—now that the poet is a wasp—he has a heart that " watches and receives :" the bee-slave toils and perishes—it is so throughout the whole industrial world; through all beedom beedom is martyrdom, it is the watching and receiving spirit that enjoys everything.

Powerful honey that must have been which was once found in the carcase of a dead lion. The strong man, the lion-slayer, said of it " out of strength came forth sweetness." Perhaps he inferred that " out of the rich depths of the strong intellect come delicious and enduring thoughts ;" or this, " out of the slain carcase of any enormity or oppression comes a divine sweetness," for

> " Sweeter than music by moonlight—more sweet
> Than daisy or buttercup, dewed at our feet,
> Is the sense of a duty performed, which the mind
> Had looked on repugnant, and fain had declined.

Really one would think that no poet could desire

his poetry to resemble bees' honey after what Shakspeare has said of it—that of it

"A little above a little is by much too much."

Golden or gem-like poetry, notwithstanding the
title, there may be none in this volume; yet the
assumption is not in me out of character, for a critic
has said that I am "self-important and pragmatical."
Can the critic change his skin, or the poet his spots?
The allegation may be true, for who knows himself?
The way to the temple of self-knowledge is through
the little wicket-gate of humility, but we so blind
ourselves with the lilies and roses of self-love we cannot find it.

Long, long ago, Miss Landon said to me with her
pen, "Perhaps a poet's best reward is a knowledge of
the pleasure he has given." Yes, truly it is; but when
we lay ourselves open to admit that breath of summer
fragrance, knats come in, buzzing and stinging, wasps,
hornets, and the whole generation of vipers. And in
the dusk of envious malignity, the owls of wisdom
hoot, and blind, booby moths blunder in to bounce
out one's poetical light.

That was my experience in the dark era of some
thirty or forty years ago; when no stone or lump of
poetical lead "with an alacrity of sinking" could go
fast enough to the bottom of Lethe without some

officious hand being hastily thrust after it. At that time dense opaque bodies of eclipse could darken the whole land betwixt author and reader.

But in this luminous age of ever-growing educational light; in this age when non-intervention is fashionable, every author is the worker-out of his own destiny, by being allowed to speak for himself in ample quotations, and to save or condemn himself in the good sense of his readers. The million no longer ask what a thing is; they neither need a good or evil name for it, but guided by their own taste, accept or reject it on their own responsibility. Modern readers are not in the condition of Sancho Panza, when every dish was forbidden to him as unwholesome. Knowledge is electrical; it flashes from mind to mind. No one can impede it; no one seeks to impede it. The generous literary dictator takes the deserving author by the hand, and makes him free of the flowery parterres, and Eden-walks of a limitless popularity.

The gates thrown open, the surly old porters, the Giffords and Dennises, dead, yet I have hesitated to enter, having been in a little way on several occasions before.

Literally the body of this book has been printed sixteen months, only waiting for this head, that it might come forth, and "walk the town awhile."

I have dated some of the poems, to shield myself
from the charge of plagiarism, as some of them have
woke remarkable echoes. I give one instance. The
" Woodland Well" has these first two lines—

> " O, the pleasant woodland well,
>   Gemmed about with roses."
>
> *Metropolitan Magazine.*

Echo " Wayside Well,"

> " Oh, the pretty wayside well,
>   Wreathed about with roses."
>
> *Household Words.*

If any are annoyed by " The Old Surplice," let
them read the character of a good clergyman in " Village Pastorals." The best churchman knows that
there are buyers and sellers in the temple ; men who
do a large, old established, and lucrative business, in
black cloth and white cravats.

Out of the abundant poetical blossoming of very
many years I have selected this small wreath ; some
of the wild-flowers from what Mr. Tennyson terms
the " under world." Life has however, other visit-
ings than the heavenly revelations of flowers or
poetry. One of these I experienced at Staplehurst ;*

---

* In the newspaper list of the names of persons more or less
injured, the one given as mine was so little like it, as to enable
me " to wear the receipt of fernseed, and to walk invisible."
Also, the village in which I reside came out of the accident with
half a *Head* more than belonged to it.

a railway tragedy made historically memorable by
Mr. Dickens being there—on the way, as it happened,
to "Mugby Junction." I have been in what at the
time seemed a more awful situation than that : in a
collision at sea in midnight storm and darkness. I
heard on that occasion the captain order two of his
boldest seamen aloft, to cut away the entanglements
which held the ships together. One of them hesitated : "Come along, Jim," called out the foremost,
" it's all one ; we shall all be in hell in five minutes !"
yet all got safe to land.

I owe much, for many deliverances by land and sea,
to a benign and merciful Providence, and would make
some return, something, albeit little. The Greek
mariner, in token of grateful deliverance, hung up his

"Dank and dripping weeds,"

in the temple of Neptune : yet I seek not to suspend
this wreath in any grand temple of British song, but
rather to place it in homely haunts and easily accessi-
ble places, that the poorest intellectual wayfarer may
gather that which I have freely received from the
Giver of every pure, graceful, good, and acceptable
gift.

Border of Sherwood Forest,
    Autumn, 1867.

CONTENTS.

CONTENTS.

xviii   CONTENTS.

PRELUDE.

———

Songs which I sung in life's sweet May,
Come back like ghosts we cannot lay :
Yet seems not one an evil sprite,
That slinks away, and fears the light.

Simple and pure, not learned, nor high,
Homely the themes, and ever nigh :
By the soul's alchymy enwrought
To glowing song, that came unsought.

I went to sea—soon there to find
Before me children of my mind ;
I found that they had power to please :
I found them at the antipodes.

The ship-boy, 'mid Brazilian foam,
Who wildly left a cultured home,
His alien anguish, 'mid the brine,
Soothed with remembered strains of mine.

Great griefs the rich man's hand can heal.
When rich men chance to think and feel :
Can largely local good provide—
But song is—as the world is—wide.

As ocean-winds wake from grim sleep,
And shake the ship o'erwhelming deep
Till terror breathes not for their breath—
And Life is wrestling hard with Death :

Song has like might—despise not song—
Alike for good and evil strong ;
'Tis life—'tis freedom—men or realms
It vivifies, or overwhelms !

When to the people of his choice
God spake—spake through the human voice,
The words were music on the tongue
Blest psalms of heaven—despise not song.

Like waves, which roll unto the shore,
Is song—that flashing are no more :
Yet where they dash, foam up, and die,
Rare gems, rich pearls, and opals lie.

BALLADS,

ETC.

~~~~~~~~~

THE BALLAD OF JOHN DALE.

A PLEASANT man was young John Dale,
　A frank man and a free:
But they who saw with pleasure John Dale,
　Will John Dale never more see.

From Winkburn, in the merry spring-time
　For Kirklington he goes:
But why he comes not to Kirklington
　There's never an old dame knows.

He lies in the wood, he lies in his blood,
　Just covered with boughs of tree:
The hare it hops by carelessly,
　The thrush it sings with glee.

1

His kin far away still see John Dale
    Move on from place to place:
For them he yet is a living man,
    They see the smile on his face.

But the old wives of Kirklington,
    They unto each other say,
" How strange it is John Dale does not come,
    For it is the market-day.

" How strange it is, and very, very strange,
    On a lovely day like this."
And they walk and talk from house to house,
    And feel there's something amiss.

For when it would blow and drift the snow,
    That there was scant any track;
The day it came, and the hour it came,
    And came John Dale with his pack.

The market-folk stream on to the town—
    They pass by the wood on the way:
They pass the wood of the deed of blood
    At noon on the market-day.

" What did you shoot at, Stanley ?"
    The market-goers cry:
" At a deer"—growled the keeper—
    And sullenly stalked by.

" O, Stanley, Stanley !" cried John Dale,
　　When feeling death's chilly dew,
" With you I played some games last night—
　　O, Stanley, is it you ?"

" With you in the old inn parlour,
　　I talked, intent on play :
And little thought that you with death
　　Would meet me here to-day !"

Now send your thoughts to a far-away place,
　　And a small cottage there see,
Wherein there dwells a fair young wife,
　　With all things orderly.

A bride there is, and a fair young bride,
　　Who thinks, and blesses her lot.
The mother to be of the fatherless,
　　A widow, and knows it not.

" And who is there like my John Dale ?"
　　She sighs—" the kind and the good."
The man through whose heart a bullet has pass'd,
　　The murdered of Wickburn-wood.

O, she shall watch through the lone summer night,
　　And weep—until tears fail :
And listen—and start—and look to see—
　　But never more see John Dale.

Deep, deep is the shade on Winkburn-wood—
    'Tis deep at the noon of day:
And when the moon shines brightest in heaven—
    Nor will ever more pass away.

Now John Dale's poor old father,
    Nor night, nor day can he rest;
But he goes north, and he goes south,
    And he goes east and west.

But vain is all his labour—
    The search doth bootless seem;
Until at length the mysterious wood
    Is shown from God in a dream.

Then forth once more he goeth—
    He searcheth the country round:
He sees the wood, and he knows it—
    And the murdered man is found.

The murderer, too, is taken:
    The blood cried from the sod.
Go!—leave the murdered man to his rest—
    And the murderer leave to God.

The vulture, Remorse, his heart is rending—
    The deed to God has arisen!
And he, who slaughtered pleasant John Dale,
    Hath strangled himself in prison!

RAILWAY SONNETS.

Rude railway-trains, with all your noise and smoke,
I love to see you wheresoe'er ye move :
Though Nature seems such trespass to reprove :
Though ye the soul of old romance provoke,
I thank you that from misery ye unyoke
Thousands of panting horses. Science pleased,
Sees by machinery lungs and sinews eased,
And Mercy smiles as sufferings ye revoke.
Calm sanctities, deem not such march profane :
Sweet meads give up your flowers and emerald sod :
Small fields resign your being without pain :
For, thinking on old roads in anguish trod,
Not to the heart of Nature can be vain
Humanity, which serves both man and God.

Lawns, shaven smooth ; parterres all summer fair,
With rarest flowers from farthest regions brought :
Groves dedicate to friendship and sweet thought :
These, touch'd by railways, wither in despair,
Die in strong light, and the obtrusive air.

For gardens, crofts, old owners are distraught,
For cottages, home-hallowed, scorned as naught;
Leisure made public, and retirement bare.
Thank God it is so. Hence, in order due,
To countless blessings these distractions tend:
Good to the million: social gifts ensue:
The anxious lover, and the heart-warm friend,
Parents and children long-lost sweets renew,—
All quickly met, as 'twere from the world's end!

Hood's Mag. 1845.

DISPARITY.

In the most famous realm of the wide world,
In Nature's sweetest land we live to hear,
The trampling of taxation, and the groans:
Then come the intervals of horrid gloom :
The workless silence, wageless misery:
Want's silent murders, which, like water-drops,
Wear men to clay.   In sunshine and sweet air
Flush wealth holds dalliance with festivity:
With dance, with song, and riotous merriment,
Keeping perpetual pother o'er the heads—
Over the world-wide dungeon of the poor!
Famine and luxury, that, like earth and sea,
Confront each other, meet, but never mix.
The poor! the poor! the trodden multitude—
What hope is there for them, the trodden poor?
The dwellers in the desert of this life :
Thrust out from life's most blest amenities :
Who still through gates of adamant, iron barred—
Catch glimpses of the paradise of wealth !
The poor! the poor! the trodden multitude—

The undergrowth of nations, which rot down,
Leaf, bud, and sickly blossom which rot down,
Where stately boles rise up into the light,
That stately boles may grow yet statelier!
O, land! with lords and beggars overrun!
O, motley land! in rags and finery decked!
Shall such disparity be thine for ever?
A lord? a lord? what delegated power
Holds he from Heaven, that he should be a lord?
Our Lord is Christ! we need none other Lord!
We need not gods and demigods of clay!
But earnest men we need, true Christian men!
O, wealth still loves to play the mountebank—
Gold has its harlequins; belted and starred—
Huge children, overgrown, of ignorance gone—
The silly pageantry of pride and power!
Put forth your hands, great lords! unto the tree
Of lasting life, grand lords! and live for ever!
What are our threescore years and ten, for you—
And by infirmities more miserable—
You! who are housed in palaces—whose path,
Flower-strewn, is through the goodliest of the earth!
Go on your way, until you feel how poor
All titles are where worth ennobles man!
But for those gates of adamant, O Christ!
Deep laid in ignorance, bastioned strong by pride,
And sentinelled by gaunt necessity—
Those gates of stern, insuperable bars,

Which sever wide the poor man and the rich,
Strew them in ruin—raise thy temple there—
Thou only Lord of severed human-kind—
Whose Sun of Love can warm them into one.
1817.

NOTE. When I wrote the above I had just seen twenty poor arti-
zans, drawing a waggon load of coals. This they did to excite public
compassion, rather than break up their homes, and go with their families into the union workhouse. The distance of the journey was fifteen
miles. Hundreds of families were in the same condition. Soon as I
had left these poor men, who by no fault of theirs, were reduced
to the sad condition of brutes—nay worse, there passed me on the
same road an earl's carriage—the men in glaring liveries—the horses
fat, sleek, and dappled, and glittering with silver.

SPRIGHTLY AND SPAVIN'S HEDGE CON-FABULATION.

You've heard horselaughs, here's some horse-talk
I overheard one day in my walk.

A SMALL white horse, smooth, silky, and fat,
Owned by a man with a rather broad hat:
A nag that he bought since his second marriage,
To trot with his bride in a low-wheeled carriage.
A fortunate beast, well-tended and neat,
With plenty of grass to sleep in and eat:
In sunshine sleeping, snorting, and playing,
Tossing his silvery mane and neighing:
Or idly full, looking into the lane,
As with some *neigh*-boor to chat he would fain.
And lo! comes limping, with scant any breath,
A poor lane-grazer, waiting for death:
Clumsy as wooden, and lumpish as lead,
Evermore dying, yet never dead:
With many a bare-rubbed hole in his skin,
Where famine and toil invite death in.
" Ha, ha!" says silky mane, with a faint neigh—
" How are you faring, old creature, to-day ?"

SPAVIN.

" Well, really, it frightens me out of my wits,
To think of the loads which I drag from those pits!
" Tis fifteen miles there, and thence I must track
That awful fifteen with that load at my back ;
Panting and weak, and Heaven well knows
Not helped on by corn, but by plenty of blows ;
Then turned out quite sinking to shift as I can,—
Such is the merciful nature of man."

SPRIGHTLY.

" The nature of *some ;* well, *our* people are kind—
And to faithfully serve them, bent is my mind.
They never go out on a party of pleasure
But I go to share it, and draw them at leisure ;
And when in the woodlands they get out their books,
They turn me to graze in the loveliest nooks,
Where brooks run and frisk it, and coil up, and sleep,
And leaf shadows tremble, and grass is knee-deep.
Those parties of pleasure though, where there are many
To fill up the carriage, I like least of any.
And yet, to do justice to such folk as they,
They get out and walk up the hills, I must say.
But, foh ! how you smell of cart-grease, my old friend,
Don't press quite so close, or our confab must end."

SPAVIN.

" Yes, yes ! my young sir, you'll be taught by-and-bye,
A thing or two when you're as ugly as I.

In youth of great kindness like you I could boast,
For I, in those days, was as handsome as most:
I lived then in clover—my master a priest—
And found in his service light labour at least.
Oh! had we the hard work when best we could do it,
Not when we can bring no ability to it!
World! world of mutations mysteriously strange,
From *that* unto *this* what a horrible change!
My master is bad, but his son is the worst—
I'm loaded and goaded, and famished and cursed!
Just roll yourself over, and leap and curvet—
A time there is coming, that's far off as yet."

SPRIGHTLY.

" You! young once and handsome—nay, now that's a
     joke,
And, but for your pain, would my laughter provoke.
All men are not tyrants—the field of our neighbour
Maintains an old horse that now rests from all labour.
And then, my old boy, I had thought us befriended,
That railways and steam had our drudgery ended:
But, may-be, directors, to show their great sense,
Have done such grand works at so vast an expense,
That cheapness is out of the question as yet,
So dear are the railways, and deeply in debt,
You're turned but from inns, where good food filled
     the racks,
But from coach-horses changed into higglers' hacks:

Well, that is too bad—you have had a sad fate—
So just of your history something relate."

SPAVIN.

" It would be too painful—and yet a slight touch
I may give you—not dwell on my miseries much.
Being liked as a horse, nigh as well as could be,
The first twenty years I had masters but three.
That priest was the kindest. Then next for some years
I drew an old lady all fidgets and fears :
She couldn't bear shaking—so I must move slow—
I did—the dread cause of my subsequent woe.
I dozed—broke my knees by a fall, and was sold,
Then thick came the horrors which scarce can be told.
The Flints and the Skinflints then wore me down fast,
And my fate was, to come to be George's at last ;
And George, after wearing out horses in swarms,
Has made money by us, and higgles and farms.
There's me and another—and still more to try us—
Though George has no mercy he thinks himself pious.
KIND ACTS WORSHIP GOD! a hawk is no pigeon—
And wolves are still wolves, though professing religion.
One Martin once tried our tormentors to awe,
By hanging out o'er them the scourge of the law !
Where wrongs are unwitnessed, enactments are vain—
A merciful bullet would best end our pain.
Depend on't—and fix this truth deep in your mind—
The villains who rob us, rob most their own kind."

SPRIGHTLY.

" O yes, I can see it—the lesson is plain,
After thirty years' toil your reward—is—a lane.
Your pasture as lean as your ribs—and, for rest,
Why, the grass in this field is nigh up to my breast;
You cannot get in, for I cannot get out,
That lane is your treadmill and Union, no doubt.
Well,—good-bye—and, old friend, the best thing I
   can say,
If I meet with kind Death, I will send him your way."

1854.

OLD JOHN BROWN.

"And let us chant a passing stave
In honour of that hero brave."—WORDSWORTH.

On Tell and Hofer's name we dwell;
  We love their just renown,
Who in the cause of freedom fell,
  And won the laurel crown.
And Wallace wight, a name of might,
  By Scotia handed down;
And many another valiant soul
  That feared no tyrant's frown:
And now we'll write on fame's rare scroll,
  The name of brave John Brown.

No foe approached his native land:
  He feared no foreign foe:
Or had been ready, hand to hand,
  To mete such blow for blow.
But the oppressed, who bore the brand
  Of slavery did he know:
And put his life into his hand
  It down for them to throw.

For them, in their sad hopeless state,
   The scorned, the trodden down,
He felt, and fought, and met his fate,
   Firm, dauntless old John Brown.

His foes unconsciously were kind,
   Who cut life's loosening thread:
But could not touch his generous mind,
   Whose influence is not dead.
The evil blindly lead the blind—
   The good man's work will spread.
In thought we see his final hour,
   And reverently bow down
In thankfulness to that Great Power,
   Who sent the oppressed, John Brown.

His manly sons, who round him fall,
   Have looks that do not cower:
The Bibles he bequeathes, are all
   As strongholds, each a Tower.
His dead still plead: his latest words
   Come forth with conquering power:
His death is worth a million swords
   For freedom's hastening hour.
For, myriads, far in deepest night,
   In wilderness and town,
Have seen broad streaks of coming light
   From sacrificed John Brown.

And when that Dragon of the South
   (Late fierce from menaced death)
Has spent the venom of his mouth,
   And spent his baleful breath :
And that dread mass, whom wrongs debase,
   Have ceased to groan and bleed :
When Man is Man whate'er his race,
   His colour, or his creed :
The race that on him fastened shame,
   And hurled to darkness down,
Will reverence the name and fame
   Of martyred brave John Brown.

Immediately on John Brown's execution this poem appeared in the "Morning Star." The dread conflict foreshadowed in it has been—and the battle of the slave fought, and won.

A USEFUL LIFE.

HE never cared for show or state,
　But to be useful most aspired:
In active life to work and wait;
　Part public life, and part retired.

But his retirement was not rest:
　No listless, aimless idler he:
But what in books and men was best
　From men and books he gathered free.

To wide extend the works of peace:
　To break the fetters of the slave:
To bid domestic light increase;
　To these his energies he gave:

To nobly stir the general soul;
　To teach the ignorant, raise the low;
And knowledge breathe throughout the whole,
　That thence good government might grow.

Thus one continued stream of good,
　From early days his years have run;
The healthful current of his blood,
　As warm and genial as the sun.

Antique his dress as it had slept
   Two centuries, yet retained its gloss:
As from the picture frame had stept
   John Howard, or the Man of Ross.

But dress was nothing to his mien:
   The Roman contour—softened, blent,
With christian suavity serene—
   Benign, and most intelligent.

And still is his life's lengthening span,
   With hoary head of honoured hairs;
And for the family of man
   He feels his old paternal cares.

Still, still is his the thoughtful head;
   And still is his the active hand,
Death is a thing he does not dread,
   Whose life is useful in the land.

No matter where his labours close:
   No matter where his ashes lie:
A breath, the odour of the rose—
   Will breathe about him from the sky.

A COUNTRY JUSTICE.

WHO MAY HAVE LIVED IN THE DARK AGES.

Born unto wealth, opposed to good,
    He exercised himself in ill;
Of old and honourable blood,
    But prone, debased in heart and will.

He gloried in his strength of frame,
    And made his will his rule of right:
But most he gloried in his shame,
    And in oppression took delight.

The poor man's rights he laughed to scorn,
    And spurned beneath his horse's hoof:
Poor wretches, not to affluence born,
    And therefore worthy of reproof.

Both men and beasts to him were game:
    And had he lived in earlier times,
When here the Norman Bastard came,
    He would have helped him in his crimes.

He would have loosely flung the reins,
    To hunt, to burn, and to subdue;
Had eyed with joy the smoking plains,
    All horrors of that Forest New.

He came where one rich rose had birth,
    In stately beauty waving free;
He plucked and trod it in the earth,
    That only rose of all the tree.

And other purity he stained:
    And trampled upon heart and head:
Till hate, all purple, swollen-veined,
    Glared, muttering execrations dread.

Two men suspended high for rape,
    Dangling at once the people saw,
With thoughts of him who could escape,
    Through wealth, that *finale* of the law.

Of him, commissioned to decide
    Of justice, which he loved the least:
Whilst some, even rich, but brutified,
    Bowed down in worship of such beast.

'Till justice, long time spurned and shamed,
    In breasts began to boil and seeth;
That men, his odious name who named,
    Spat out, and firmlier fixed their teeth.

'Till popular hatred raged aloud,
    And rushed in one impetuous flood:
And men, with weapons in the crowd,
    Had fain avenged them in his blood.

But wherefore? why should men presume
   God's justice-bolts to grasp and sway,
Who had appointed him his doom,
   Far off, the vengeance and the day?

Most awful were his closing hours,
   A household terror, 'till there grew
A peace about those ancient towers,
   As late his loathèd life withdrew.

Coffin'd and hears'd, with followers few;
   Hurried and jolted far and fast,
The dead received the honours due,
   Like refuse forth to darkness cast.

I ask not where his bones repose,
   In dirt or marble, foul or fair;
Nor where the noisome fungus grows,
   Or spotted hemlock taints the air.

BALLAD.

Most beautiful and blest the spot
　　Where Lucy had her dwelling,
The lovely lass of Avondale—
　　All other maids excelling.
To every place she lent a grace,
　　The light was glad about her;
Her cottage neat, so flowery sweet,
　　No home had been without her.

Her cheeks made poor the rose of June—
　　Hers was the daisy's neatness:
She moved, the cowslip of the mead;
　　The violet's was her sweetness.
But most did tranquil Avon show
　　The charm which made you love her,
For in herself did she reflect
　　The heaven that was above her.

Her brows were clear as orient skies—
　　Hair dark as clouds of thunder—
But the sweet lightning of her eyes
　　Awoke surprise and wonder.

Beloved was she by many youths,
  Both brave and comely many :
But though she scorned not any one,
  She did not wed with any.

So easy were her manners sweet,
  Each lover thought to win her :
But the sweet lass of Avondale
  A powerful soul had in her.
But little saw she of the rich,
  But little was her reading,
Yet shewed her mind a sense refined,
  Her manners nicest breeding.

So sweetly blent she in her looks
  The serious and the simple ;
The liveliest thoughts played round her mouth,
  Arch grace in every dimple.
She stilled the pert, she awed the bold,
  Such sweet reserve came o'er her ;
And when the boldest sought her love,
  They stood abashed before her.

At length upon a sick bed long
  Sweet Avon's lass was lying ;
And her fond parents o'er her hung,
  With thoughts that she was dying,—

When came a youth unto her side,
    Whose loving zeal amazed her ;
And her pale cheeks with blushes dyed,
    So tenderly he praised her.

Then might in her a strife be seen,
    The filial and the tender,
And will habitual to refuse,
    Unwilling to surrender.
At length she put the youth aside,
    Without one kindly token,
And half the love within his heart
    Died from his lips unspoken.

But from that day did she amend,
    Nor would she wed another :
And now the lass of Avondale
    Is blest, as wife and mother.
For never did she disesteem
    Plain path and homely duty,
And humblest household offices
    Seem hallowed by her beauty.

REGRETS FOR SHERWOOD FOREST.

Alas! for old Sherwood, for upland and glade,
   And streams in wild liberty flowing;
Stern ruin frowns o'er them with axe and with spade,
   Whilst Robin Hood sleeps all unknowing.

Yet seems it enough from his grave in Kirklees,
   To rouse him with bow and with quiver,
Or make him turn over as ill at his ease,
   That his Forest must vanish for ever.

Methinks I see Scarlett, Will Stutely, and John,
   And Tuck, smit with sensible horror:
And Marian for ever ride weeping, as one
   In a deep inconsolable sorrow.

Wild creatures the doom of their old haunts lament;
   Each stream's a disconsolate lover;
And sighs from the heart of the forest are sent
   That its old primal grandeur is over.

Mansfield bells, once so merry, seem troubled with grief,
   Or else with age palsied and dizzy:
Once joyous to Robin, as courteous a thief,
   As e'er in the greenwood was busy.

Alas, for old oaks, that must perish ere long,
 The bald, the stag-antlered and hoary:
That once were so graceful, so burly, and strong,
 When outlaws roamed here in their glory.

Ye forest-destroyers! linger and pause,
 Good, public and private pursuing;
Oh! war not with Nature's beneficent laws,
 Nor blend useless beauty in ruin.

Not useless the beauty of sterile and wild—
 Let Time yet some portion inherit!
Where Nature may walk hand-in-hand with her child,
 And nurse him in freedom of spirit.

THE BOY FORESHOWS THE MAN.

Behold that young imp of a boy,
  He can't his propensity smother;
But selfishly grasps at the toy,
  The plaything that pleases his brother.
Depend on't when older and stronger,
  He'll make his weak father a will;
Lands, houses he'll grasp in his hunger,—
  A hunger that nothing can fill.

His mother has striven, and striven,
  His nature to change or control,
But spite of the washings she's given,
  The black-a-moor-stain 's in his soul.
'Tis only like checking a river,
  To rob but more fields in its way:
The impulse is with him for ever;
  And thieving is sweeter than play.

And yet with less pain I behold him
  A thief—not a hypocrite too;
Some cloak will hereafter enfold him,
  Plain robbery never will do.
The world yet more cunning will make him;
  He'll watch for his prey out of sight:
Then when in his jungle you wake him,
  'Twill be for a spring and a bite.

MERRY HUGH; OR, THE LIBERTINE'S LESSON.

IN TWO FIXES.

He thought to defile a virtuous bed,
But stepped into a tomb instead.

FIX THE FIRST—*COMIC.*

A MERRY little fellow was Hugh,
  In whom not yet affliction had wrought,
With agonies piercing through and through,
  Much serious thought.

He and Care were never a pair,
  Soon they parted whenever they met:
He supped not with sorrow, nor cared for the morrow,
  Nor chewed the cud of regret.

But well 'tis known that a broken bone,
  It may be a rib or a shin,
Will set the wheels of the brain a-spinning,
  And somehow let light in.

Others find a knock on the mind,
  Some passion aroused in might,
Has power to couch the morally blind,
  And let in painful light.

Even so it chanced unto merry Hugh,
   Of whom we are singing this stave;
An agony came which pierced him through,
   And made him feel very grave.

A man he was of mutable moods,
   Compounded like April weather;
Or like shallow streams that shine and brawl—
   He laughed and he wept together.

He roved wherever his fancy led—
   His prime delight was a Fair;
And to a wake his way he would take,
   As though his home lay there.

On many a night 'twas his delight,
   When meditating sin,
If he chanced to roam, to make his home
   In a quiet country inn.

One such he found, one October eve,
   Far down in the vale of the Trent,
" This Dog and Pheasant," said he, " seems pleasant"—
   And into the inn he went.

Now jaunty Hugh the house strolled through,
   The kitchen, the tap, and the bar;
But most bewitching appeared the kitchen,
   He liked it the best by far.

Oh! oh! he liked the kitchen the most,
    And fixed himself down on the settle,
For there he saw the buttered toast,
    And heard the song of the kettle.

And more, oh, more, enchantingly more,
    In air, in form, and in feature,
The hostess who leant the tea-table o'er,
    Was a most loveable creature.

" How's this, fair hostess, are you alone—
    Pray where is good Antony Vincke ?"
(He merely had read the name on the sign,)
    " For with him this night I would drink."

" My husband is gone to Newark, sir,
    And may-be returns not to-night."
" If that be true," quoth merry Hugh,
    " I am very sure it is right :

" For here this night must be my inn—
    For a bed I must be your debtor ;
And were it your own to which I was shown,
    I should like it all the better."

Oh, Hugh! oh, Hugh! vain, frivolous Hugh,
    Is this a place for such vice ?
The house it is clean, is most painfully clean,
    And the hostess is neat and is nice.

The hostess frowned—but ere long agreed,
   With a most innocent face,
As though to do her husband that wrong
   Were neither sin nor disgrace.

Little Hugh smoked, and little Hugh quaffed,
   And chuckled over his glass,
And thought the sweet young wife of the inn
   A blithe kind-hearted lass.

Merry Hugh laughed, and merry Hugh sang,
   As blithe as a lark in May;
For why?—because he knew not yet
   What reckoning he should pay.

Old stories told Hugh, old stories and new,
   Humming and brisk as a bee;
And it seemed the gay young wife of the inn
   Was just as merry as he.

A time or two came a step to the door,
   Or else the mice stirred on the shelves;
But strange as it seemed, no neighbour dropped in,
   The two had the house to themselves.

At length the dame caught up the candle,
   And showed him the way to her nest,
And promised when doors and windows were barred,
   To come, and to make him blest.

" There's many a slip 'twixt the cup and the lip,"
　　It hath been said and sung;
And now there came a rap at the door,
　　With which the whole house rung.

Our hero stood, one foot in the bed,
　　Of all his clothes undight;
When up ran the hostess wringing her hands,
　　And looking half dead with affright.

"My husband is here, alack! alack!—
　　And though to part I am loth;
Yet, were he to find you here in my bed,
　　I'm sure he would murder us both.

" Out, out at this window, 'tis not far down—
　　Nay stay not to dress, dispatch!
And I will drop your clothes after you
　　Down on the pigsty thatch."

Down dropped Hugh on the pigsty thatch—
　　Right glad to be so quit:
But for the clothes that he was to catch,
　　He had to wait a bit.

He heard the window go to with a smack,
　　And all was silent after,
Save that he thought he heard in the house
　　A merry peal of laughter.

O, Hugh! O Hugh! ridiculous Hugh!
    To turn out thus in your buff,
When the night air was cutting and raw,
    And the night wind it was rough.

"That woman-beast," groaned Hugh, "and her mate,
    My money and clothes have got;
And thus to come at my money and clothes,
    Was this a most devilish plot."

Now Hugh he shrunk, and crouched in the cold,
    And then he swore and he wept,
And then down from the pigsty thatch
    With a cautious foot he stepped.

Old mother earth was a comfortless berth,
    And he touched with a tremulous start,
His new acquaintance the bare-foot earth—
    A cold that leapt at his heart.

At length he made up his mind, 'twas vain
    To linger after such pillage;
So on he crept, and onward he stept,
    Then scampered away through the village.

On, on he went, with mud besprent,
    Past lonely farm and wood;
And if he scared some women to death,
    He also did some good.

For it is said, men out of bed
  There were, in a drunken plight,
Who, as white Hugh came into view,
  Grew sober at the sight.

And who, for many years afterwards,
  Did much surprise their wives,
By staying quietly at home
  And leading regular lives.

Now what became of poor little Hugh,
  And how his home he gained,
With a *little* delay that he met by the way,
  Will be hereafter explained.

FIX THE SECOND—*TRAGI-COMIC.*

" Past twelve o'clock," the watchmen bawled,
  When Hugh gained his native town:
Where, shunning those sentries, he popped through
    entries,
  Threading them up and down.

He went by the church of St. Mary,
  Just to cut shorter the way;
And there through the porch he saw in the church
  A light which caused him to stay.

Thought Hugh, the body-snatchers are here
   Busy at their vocation,
And I will unto them appear,
   To give them a sensation.

So temptingly stood the door ajar,
   Our hero could not but enter;
And there he saw two ruffianly men,
   By a stone reared up in the centre.

Hugh saw them, and they saw Hugh,
   Their hair with horror uprising—
For, thinking the devil walked not in white,
   The visit was most surprising.

Here they looked, and there they looked,
   In awe-struck trepidation:
Ready to catch at the slightest chance
   Of instant evaporation.

But on came Hugh 'twixt them and the door,
   Which barred all chance of escaping:
So there they stood with horrent hair,
   Loose-kneed, with mouths wide-gaping.

" I am no ghost, good fellows," cried Hugh,
   " I've only been robbed of my dress,
And so I made free to come to you,
   For help in my distress."

"If that be all," said one well pleased,
  "Come hither, and go down below;
Only just hand us the body out,
  And we'll clothe you from top to toe."

Now Hugh went down without any demur,
  Although he felt some loathing;
But what in the world could a poor fellow do—
  So wretchedly off for clothing?

A rough blow or two, and the coffin-lid flew—
  When, looking on what lay under,
A step, a moment he back withdrew,
  Surprised by the sleeping wonder.

As sculpture fair, a girl of thirteen,
  That less seemed dead than dozing:
Like that in the church of Ashbourne seen,
  Immortally reposing.

O, grief! she had slept in cosiest state,
  In robes ambrosial enfolden;
Where mother's tears fell early and late,
  O'er tresses auburn-golden.

And now, O shame! with horridest hent,
  By wretches that mutter and scamper,
Her dainty limbs will be handled and bent,
  And brutally jammed in a hamper.

Hugh fain would have spared the beautiful dead,
  As conscience began to awaken;
But at thought of the villains over his head,
  And what he had undertaken:

He handily handed the body out,
  When, down went the stone with a snap;
And there was Hugh, poor pitiful Hugh,
  Shut up in a horrible trap.

Poor Hugh, poor Hugh! what now could he do,
  Smit all on a heap with amazement,
On finding this affair of the vault,
  Much worse than that of the casement?

The laughter he heard in the inn was light,
  Compared with the fiendish laughter,
Which rung through the nave, and swelled through
    the roof,
  Dying down distantly after.

Little he thought the dress which they meant,
  Would prove a final engravement,
A jerkin of brick enfolding him quick,
  And capt with impassable pavement.

Hugh flung himself down on the sepulchre floor,
  In agonized desperation,
And smashed to dust old coffins which held
  The bones of the past generation.

But calmer at length, he put forth his strength,
   He tried with might and with main,
To heave with his back the stone from the vault,
   But Hugh he tried in vain.

He heaved till the nerves of his eye-balls cracked,
   And his eyes swelled large in his head:
And he seemed to see a thousand ways,
   Cold stony eyes of the dead.

The air was noisome, and close, and damp:
   And ever more seemed to arise,
As though the dead were not thoroughly dead,
   Sad, low, sepulchral sighs.

Now high in the grey old monkish tower,
   The sullen clock struck one:
And down through the ground came the quivering
     sound,
   Surging, and surging on.

"O, God!" sighed Hugh, "a sinner am I,
   And terrible is my doom;
Here shut up am I, by inches to die,
   Deep buried alive in this tomb."

And then he prayed, and groaned, and wept:
   "But hist!" thought Hugh, "can it be,
That the villains are coming back to the vault,
   For my body to murder me?

" Or haply the corse which I handed out,
　Might die of some strange disease:
And other doctors look after it,
　As keenly as after their fees."

Most vividly were Hugh's senses awake:
　His ear caught the lightest sound:
And now was he sure of approaching steps,
　Heard far on the hollow ground.

He heard the hinge of the old church door:
　Then voices of men unknown:
Then a heavier tread the way that led,
　Right on to the sepulchre stone.

Again and again was the crow-bar tried:
　Up wearily rose the stone:
And Hugh, ready-witted—rose up into sight—
　And breathed forth a dolorous groan.

They staggered—they stood—bewildered, aghast:
　Then off like a whirlwind they flew:
Whilst lighter with joy than they were with fear,
　Quick after them danced Hugh.

A few minutes more, and Hugh reached his door,
　Knock'd—and was soon let in:
And soon snug in bed to himself he said—
　" Strange suffering follows sin!

" Whoever may strive by vice to thrive,
    Will be in the sequel out-witted :
For sorrow still dogs the heels of sin,
    Intended, or committed."

In the morn to Hugh a bundle there came ;
    Cried he, " Egad on my life,
My money and clothes are all of them here,
    Sent back by that innkeeper's wife."

Our hero *was* to the hostess known,
    Although he knew her not :
And now from the bundle he drew forth a scroll,
    To read what there he had got.

" We hope the night air didn't do you much harm,
    As you would be warm with the run :
And what you got here you are welcomer to,
    Than we think we are to the fun."

Hugh blushed : and resolved for the time to come,
    That he would be circumspect, very :
And thence was more thoughtful, a wiser man,
    Though still much inclined to be merry.

THE OLD YEAR AND THE NEW.

THE old king lies in a feeble state—
    The youthful heir looks anxiously on :
But though the hour is wearing late,
    The breath from his body is not yet gone.

The young king gazeth upon the old—
    The old king has a husky speech—
And thinking the old year's days are told,
    The youth to the crown his hand doth reach.

Stay—the old king is aware of the wrong—
    It gives to his nerves and his heart a shock ;
And up he would rise, for the moment strong,
    But now it is twelve by the minster clock.

And now discrowned is the dead year alone—
    The waning moon hangs over him dim ;
For life and power with the young king are flown,
    Where kingdom and honours all wait on him.

Nay, not alone is the dead monarch laid,
    Regrets and remorse are near him found—
Behind him are shadows of ages decayed,
    Whilst memory saddens and darkens around.

A sigh there comes from the leafless woods.
 And hamlets and cities the whole world o'er.
From heath and forest, and fields and floods,
 For a time that has been, to be no more.

But now the people press nigh the throne,
 Where hushed as one are the millions still—
That what the old year has left may be known,
 For now they open and read the will.

They read of a gainful trade and a good—
 Of commerce more ample from shore to shore;
Of oil and wine, to brisken the blood—
 Of garnered grain, and of gold good store.

But yet, by folly or madness bred,
 Some national items of waste there are:
Of widows pinched for a warrior dead,
 And poor men robbed for a Kaffir war.

Then hail to thee, New Year! our eyes
 Desire thee as best life and light,
For taught by time thou wilt be more wise,
 A sovereign of more peaceful might.

O! taught by time thou wilt be more wise—
 Wiser, O! wiser, thou wilt become;
And love, from peace, God's incense will rise,
 From heart and hearth, from altar and home!

December 31, 1852.

STANZAS.

My thoughts range back through fifty years,
  Of life's first friends how few to find:
Whilst griefs that would have gush'd in tears,
  More lightly touch the chasten'd mind.
In mellow age did some depart,
  With tranquil eve and golden sun:
But more with all their wealth of heart,
  'Ere half the race of life was run.

The boughs through which was heard the storm—
  A sheltering tree away is rent.
A heart that other hearts could warm,
  Its vital current now has spent.
Down comes the irrevocable doom—
  Affection's strongholds are laid bare;
And thence there is a lonelier room,
  A lonelier hearth, and vacant chair.

All adverse strife no longer stirs,
  All sense of bitter wrongs is fled:
And fancy, touched by death, recurs
  Alone to traits that graced the dead.

Another and another sinks,
    The rending of all mortal ties:
Another and another links
    Us with the life that never dies.

Long shadows stretch athwart the grass—
    Blent with the last faint hues of day:
But by degrees the colours pass
    Till all is dim and saddest grey.
And stars come out, that lead the soul,
    To muse on mansions high and pure:
Beyond the earth and time's control—
    Where all is calm, and blest, and sure.

SIR FRANCIS LEKE; OR, THE POWER OF LOVE.

A DERBYSHIRE CATHOLIC LEGEND OF CROMWELL'S TIME.

PART I.

" O, SAY not so, Sir Francis,
　　Breathe not such woe to me,
Broad and pleasant are your lands,
　　And your Hall is fair to see.

Faithful servants have you many,
　　Fortune fair on you attends;
Nor hath Knight in all the Island,
　　Braver followers or friends.

With the Court you are a favourite—
　　Yet your King shall righted be;
In his hour of deadly peril
　　Can you from your monarch flee?

Look upon your blooming children,
　　Flowers of Heaven newly blown!
Here renewed behold your Lucy,
　　And that boy is all your own.

Shall we in these dread commotions,
    Neither need your arm nor mind,
Where shall I behold defender,
    Where shall these a father find?

How I thought you loved us! Never
    Lightly could such love decline;
Nor could you to idly voyage,
    All the wealth of life resign."

" Lucy! this is only torture—
    Here I may no longer pause—
Long I for my King have battled—
    Now we've neither King nor laws.

With our shrewd exultant Victor,
    Bootless now were strife of steel;
Looking on my bleeding country
    Can I for her cease to feel?

All the land is grown outrageous:
    Honour, worth, are hunted down:
Demons mock at our religion—
    Idiots trample on the Crown.

Roaming o'er the billowy ocean,
    Peace may greet me here unknown;
And, returning, civil tempests
    May be fairly overblown.

Should aught menacing approach you,
  To your noble Brothers look;
Danger! did they ever dread it?
  Insult! did they ever brook?

Guard your precious life, my Lucy!
  Need I say—not your's alone!
Present—absent—living—dying—
  I am—fear not—all your own!"

Starting from her arms, Sir Francis
  Quick his noble steed bestrode:
And with manly face averted,
  Forward—seaward—fleetly rode.

Soon his vessel, anchor weighing,
  To the sails the winds were true;
And with sad, not weak, delaying,
  He bade his native land adieu!

PART II.

Far amidst the western ocean,
  Lies a small and pleasant Isle;
Fair with everlasting verdure,
  Bright with summer's endless smile.

There o'er one, all sadly musing,
   Sweets distil from spicy trees;
Yet, though all around is blooming,
   Nothing cheers him that he sees.

Lonely in sweet groves of myrtle,
   Sad amongst the orange bloom;
Nothing cheers his drooping spirit,
   Nothing dissipates his gloom.

Twice ten years he there has wandered,
   Nor one human face has seen;
Moving like a silent shadow,
   Rocks have his companions been.

Clad in skins of beasts; like serpents
   Wild, is his unheeded hair;
Yet through lines of deep dejection,
   His once manly face is fair.

As from gathered flowers, the odour
   Never wholly dies away,—
Of the warrior and the scholar
   Intimations round him play.

Nurtured in the camp, the college,
   Never can his soul be void;
In the busy past his spirit,
   Heart, and mind, must be employed.

Lists he yet the stirring battle,
     Lists he Victory's rending shout?
Tranquil is the Isle, the Ocean,
     Pain within him, peace without.

Yes! he oft-times hears the trumpet,
     Captains' shouting, horses' neigh!
Till before the horrid stillness,
     All the tumult dies away.

And is this the courtly warrior,
     Gallant, gay Sir Francis Leke?
He, the same!—who shunning discord,
     Found a peace he did not seek.

Bravely sailed he from Old England,
     Boldly with adventurous prow;
From the horrors of that voyage
     He alone is living now.

To his bravery owes he being—
     Last to quit the groaning deck—
In his sight his comrades perished—
     Days he floated on the wreck.

Till this lone and lovely island
     Cheered him with refreshing bloom;
Saved him from the ravening ocean,
     To a sad and lingering doom.

In a cave has he his dwelling,
  High, o'erlooking wide the main,
Where he feeds in painful being,
  Longings infinite and vain.

Nightly there he burns a beacon;
  Often there the day he spends;
And towards his native country
  Wistful gaze o'er ocean sends.

There a cross has he erected—
  Near to which an altar stands,
Humble growth of feelings holy,
  Reared by his unaided hands.

Truly needs he prove a Christian,
  Thus cut off from all his kind;
Firmest faith he needs in Heaven;
  And boundless fortitude of mind.

Store he needs of endless knowledge,
  His unvaried hours to cheer;
Furnished with sublime resources
  For this solitude austere.

Still the Isle is very lovely—
  Never yet in Poet's mind,
Haunt of Peri, realm of faéry,
  Was more lavishly divined.

4—2

Lovely as the Primal Garden.
In the light of Sabbath blest;
Human love alone is wanting
In this Eden of the West.

Leap from rocks the living waters;
Hang delicious fruits around;
And all birds of gorgeous plumage
Fill the air with happy sound.

Painful is to him its beauty—
Sad the splendour of the sun ;
To the odorous air he utters
Sorrow, that is never done :—

" Blest was I beyond all blessing !
In my wife and children blest :
In my friends and in my fortune—
Yet in peace I could not rest.

" Never in his prosperous greatness,
Can himself the wisest trust ;
God has weighed and found me wanting—
And the punishment is just."

Oft before the cross, the altar,
Murmuring prayer he sinks to rest ;
To his God, and to his Saviour—
And the Virgin Mother blest.

And for love unto the Virgin
  Finds in Heaven his prayer chief grace;
" Mary, Mother, me deliver,
  From the horrors of this place!

" Others crave more worldly guerdon—
  Wealth, or fame, or station high;
Love I seek—to see my country—
  My own people—and to die!"

Praying thus, old legends tell us,
  Scarce his eyes in sleep were sealed;
When, O happy inward vision!
  To him was his home revealed.

There his patrimonial mansion,
  He beheld in moonlight sleep,
Saw with joy, though mystery veiled it—
  Sadness, and a silence deep.

And, O miracle of gladness!
  More, those ancient legends say,
Was permitted him to witness,
  Waking in the open day.

In his old church-porch awaking—
  Trance, or voyage all unknown;
O'er his own domains he wandered—
  Saw, and knew them for his own.

Had chance voyagers beheld him,
   In a trance, who slumbering bore,
By some heavenly impulse, guided
   Him unto his native shore?

Not so—says the holy legend—
   Force of penitential prayer—
And the love he bore the Virgin—
   Won for him that transit fair.

Spare the legend for its beauty—
   Carp not—what is it to you
If the letter is a fable?
   In its spirit it is true.

Leave we unto old tradition
   That which its dim mist sublimes,
Nor submit the ancient spirit
   To the lights of later times!

See! before his welcome threshold!
   Once again, Sir Francis stand:
Oh, the transport,—it is real!—
   He is in his native land!

PART III.

Merry once again is England,
  Civil warfare is forgot ;
Now another Charles is reigning,
  Plenty smiles in hall and cot.

Spring is like a present angel ;
  Loosened waters leap in light :
Flowers are springing, birds are singing,
  All the world is glad and bright.

May, the blue-eyed bloomy creature,
  From God's presence yearly sent,
Works with sweet ethereal fingers,
  Till both Heaven and earth are blent.

Loveliest is a rural village
  In the May-time of the year ;
With its hall, its woods and waters,
  Verdant slopes, and herds of deer.

And in one, joy is exultant—
  For this day the manly heir
Of Sir Francis Leke is wedded—
  Wedded too, his daughter fair.

Age rejoices; in the mansion
    Rural hinds find wassail cheer;
And bright troops of knights and ladies,
    Crowd the hall from far and near.

Who is this in weeds unseemly,
    Half a man that seems, half beast,
Who obtrudes himself unbidden
    On the merry marriage feast?

Hermit is he, or some pilgrim,
    Entering boldly his own cell?
No,—he lacks those ancient symbols,
    Sandal-shoon, and scallop-shell.

All the youngsters titter; anger
    Flushes cheeks austere and cold:
Whilst the aged look complacent
    On a beggar that is bold.

" Bear this ring unto your mistress,
    To a page Sir Francis cried;
And his words, emphatic uttered,
    Rung throughout the dwelling wide.

One there is—an age-blind servant—
    Who in darkness sits apart—
Carried forth to feel the sunshine—
    She has heard him in her heart;

And in agony of gladness,
 At that voice so long desired,
She has loudly named her master—
 And then instantly expired.

Pensive in her room, the matron
 Grieved—but distant from the crowd;
She would not with selfish sorrow
 Their bright countenances cloud.

There her ring receiving; Lucy
 Knew the sender of her gift,
And, it seemed, by feet unaided,
 To him she descended swift.

There upon the rugged stranger,
 Gazed, with momentary check,
Gazed—but for a passing moment,
 And then fell upon his neck.

Twice ten weary summers absent;
 By his faithful wife deplored;
Like Ulysses to his consort,
 Good Sir Francis is restored.

'Tis a time of double gladness—
 Never was a scene like this;
Joy o'erflows the hall, the village—
 'Tis a time of boundless bliss!

Clothed as instantly became him,
    Of vile skins all disarrayed,
In his old paternal mansion
    He is honoured and obeyed.

All he prayed for to the Virgin,
    She has granted him, and more;
Not to die, his own beholding,
    First, when on his native shore.

Added years of happy ending,
    Are accorded him of right ;
Midst a cloud of friends descending,
    In a sunset warm and bright.

June, 1860.

YOUTH SELF-GLORIFIED.

O, EMILY! dear Emily, the morning of our days,
Is like the lark that soars to heaven, all happiness and
    praise:
The earth is full of beauty, rose-bloom is on the sky;
And hope can never fail us, and love can never die.

O, Emily! blest Emily, the rivers we behold,
In youth seem liquid diamond, that flow o'er sands of
    gold:
So joyous is their motion, so beautiful their sleep,
That seldom think we how they tend unto the solemn
    deep.

Yet, Emily, gay Emily, dread passing bells will toll;
And change and death of those we love, fling sadness
    on the soul.
Long shadows of the evening-time will reach us ere
    the night,
Where roses bloom in maiden joy, and lilies laugh in
    light.

Then Emily, wise Emily, enjoy these blessed years,
Whilst cares are slight, and laughter light, and April-
 bright the tears :
Leave evil to its future day, sufficient it will be,
Though many are the loving hearts will wish it small
 for thee.

 1817.

RANDOM SHAFTS.

CHILDHOOD's innocent replies
Often take us by surprise;
Stir us so to thought or laughter,
They recur in years long after.

As in shallow streams seen nearly,
Smallest pebbles shine out clearly :
Spots of light from bubbles straying,
All the inner depths displaying.

Gravity of fourscore years,
Half in mirth and half in tears,
Sits, as their quick sallies smite,
Founts of pathos or delight.

Small chance arrows hit the mark,
Where old intellects are dark :
Oft discoverers of the true,
With freshness and with feelings new.

Sometimes with a sudden flash—
Done as by a random dash,

Coiled up life unrolled we see,
All that the future man will be.

At once the embryo flower is blown:
The stem at once maturely grown:
At once we see the brownest shade,
Not tint on tint as years are laid.

VILLAGE PASTORALS.

I.

THE VICAR MISPLACED.

STRANGER.

What pile is that, I pray you tell,
Round which clamour the starling and daw?

VILLAGER.

Gothic and dark, with a monkish bell,
Intended the people to overawe:
A place where the flock is fleeced right well,
And made religious according to law.

STRANGER.

I see how it is—I do not doubt it—
The priest there preaches one day in seven:
I see the dead are buried about it;
They trusted in him, and hoped for heaven.

VILLAGER.

A merciful God must be their boot,
Or fearful thoughts we must have for *them*;
For where there's rottenness at the root,
But little good can come of the stem.

STRANGER.

But teaches he not -has he no school—
　Whereby to better the next generation?

VILLAGER.

Yes! yes! he canes the head of the fool,
　And hopes, through pious flagellation,
To raise in him by regular rule,
　For church and priest great veneration.

STRANGER.

The flock is ruined by such as he—
　Who o'er the wall leap into the fold:
Pastors that porters were meant to be,
　But changed to priests by the power of gold.

Good respectable men of straw,
　Strong with musk and proud gentility:
Men correct in the moral law,
　And able to preach with neat ability.

Good friend—good friend—time out of mind,
　Pastors were fat, and sleek, and rich:
And it seems " the blind will lead the blind"—
　Till church and priest fall into the ditch.

THE OLD PRIEST AND THE NEW.

II.

STRANGER.

I PASSED through this village oft seasons ago,
And knowing it then I now seem not to know:
Of rude wayside idlers I now see not one—
Pray, where are the vice and the wretchedness gone?

The Primitive's chapel, a chapel no more,
A barn has become, as it once was before:
Where, for rant and for cant, that would quaver around,
The rational flail makes a sensible sound.

The free-school, long empty, a different place,
New glazed, is re-touched with a moderner grace:
'Twas the home of the bat; but now hark! 'tis alive,
With an under-toned hum, as from bees in a hive.

The village throughout has a pleasanter air:
Whilst the homes of the poorest show culture and care:
Pray tell me, good villager, whence is all this?
All the good I perceive, all the evil I miss?

VILLAGER.

In only one thing is the difference found—
Our stately old vicar is laid in the ground:
He went—and we bade him a thankful adieu,
But hail'd with warm greetings our vicar the new.

5

The first was seen seldom except in his coach;
A priest far too grand for poor men to approach:
A reverent justice, tenacious of power,
Most lordly in manner, in aspect most sour.

The poor and the lowly, he was not for them,
The fruit-laden bough had too lofty a stem:
Whilst the modest and worthy still found in his breath,
The freezings of winter, the March-dust of death.

His voice in the pulpit came far-off and low,
His meaning few knew it, nor cared they to know;
Our new one—God bless him! he enters your door—
His feet on the earth find the homes of the poor.

His wife and his daughters too, see! are all out:
And no one who knows them their mission will doubt;
The sad will be solaced, the hungry be fed;
The dying will bless them, be blessed the dead.

The flock are their kindred, the living a trust:
The priest is Christ's steward, and means to be just:
While he prays for the soul, for the body he cares:
And the poor feel him earnest in needful affairs.

We once went to church as a formal concern:
We now have an impulse, we listen and learn:
From the ice of dull pride melts the penitent tear:
Blind Justice has vanish'd—meek Mercy is here.

No more seems the pulpit the centre of cold,
Dropping snow-flakes of fashion on young and on old:
The winter is over—the ice-winds depart;
And the plant of the church blooms with flowers of the
    heart.

Cold, cold in his earth-bed the old vicar lies!
But I firmly believe when our new vicar dies,
The ground will be warm, as when sunsets go down:
And a glory like Christ's his true servant will crown.

STRANGER.

Good, good! I your church now must pause to admire
The graceful old porch, tall and tapering spire:
The walks and the graves, how exceedingly neat!
And methinks that the chime of these bells is most sweet!

REGRETS FOR JUNE.

I'm sorry, dear June! that thou art gone,
Though thy sun at times too fervidly shone.
Thou month of Roses wild and sweet,
Whose petals now lie in the grass at our feet.
Whose deep grass sways and curls like the sea,—
O, many a boon we owe unto thee!
Month of the early and lingering light!
Of the dry warm turf, and the balmy night;
Crown of the year, and Nature's delight!
I'm sorry, sweet June, thy season is over—
Kind month of blossoming beans and clover.
I grieve to July thy being must yield,
With sadder hues on hedge and on field;
Whilst the whetted scythe as we make it ring,
Cries "gone is the Spring! gone is the Spring!"
Gone are the days so precious and few,
A time which I then but imperfectly knew.
And the sense to my mind with sadness is fraught,
That I prized not the season half as I ought.
'Tis true that I cherished it all that I could,
With its verdure deep in valley and wood:
The wealth and the grace of its gems in the dew,
Now to feel how its value in part I but knew.

I plucked its sweets in copse and in glen
And hauntings of Eden were with me then.
I called them the gladness and beauty of youth,
The Light of Life and the Rays of Truth.
Bright rays of the sward, that sprang into birth,
As the smile of Jehovah illumin'd the earth!
And are they not these, and more than these?
That laugh with the sun, and dance with the breeze.
They come with a mission of love from on high:
Of goodness they tell us that never can die.
Beauty may flee, as beauty has fled,
But odours will live when the flowers are dead.
Therefore, thou season precious and sweet!
Though thy Roses lie dead in the grass at my feet:
Thou hast pass'd from the *outward* into the soul—
And now of thy value I feel the whole.
To know thee, whilst here, was a vain endeavour—
But now thou hast passed the bourne of *for ever*,
Thou art set apart in a heavenly light—
For Death is the teacher that teaches aright.
A memory thou! as the best must be,
And so I no more will be sad for thee:
For things of the Soul are precious if pure—
And more than for one brief season endure!

1847.

SONNET.

TO WILLIAM HOWITT.

In Germany, our old ancestral land,
Long have you dwelt, thence richest lore to bring,
Quaffing our inspirations at their spring:
Nor less, on all our glorious spots to stand,
Our Britain have you traversed staff in hand.
Aloud of Austral gold all regions ring—
Thither have thousands rushed on wildest wing,—
You, too, went forth with that adventurous band.
How men go to that Jericho, to fall
Into the robber's or the reptile's den:
How the shrine-makers golden calves enthral:
How golden pit-falls there are dug for men,
To you is known, the good, the evil, all,
And you will blazon with bold honest pen.

THE AUNT-MOTHER; OR, EASE-MISERY.

A BALLAD.

Wealthily upon the farm,
　　Rich in endless harvest sheaves;
Stealthily upon the farm,
　　Her rich lover she receives.

He is rich, and very rich,
　　Such a one could she deny?
She was poor, and very poor,
　　But she had a winning eye.

Graceful as a May-day queen:
　　Beautiful in form and face;
She was in a cottage seen,
　　Who might any mansion grace.

Caught she from some Lady Juliet
　　Manners, crowning charms like these?
And--alas! for homely duties,
　　Wealthy tastes, and love of ease.

For her parents' labour only
   Kept sure coming want at bay :
Whilst the dread divorcing Union,
   For old age, before them lay.

From a farming race descended :
   Lost the farm, depressed the race ;
Back their loving memories tended
   To one blessed time and place.

Then there came a friendly squire,
   Rich, and him they generous thought,
When he waked the heart's desire,
   And the ample farm was bought.

But one shameful reservation
   Locked he closely in his breast,
Hidden from the ancient people,
   As was for his purpose best.

In the starlight, in the moonlight,
   In long shadows of the west ;
In the farm's thick bower of roses,
   And still walks, to be confessed.

Close they step beneath the woodbines,
   Where the frail rose-petals fall :
Pathways strewing—O, the ruin,—
   Steps they never may recall.

Thence they seek the county races :
　　Dance too at the county ball :
Where amongst the high-born ladies,
　　She the loveliest is of all.

Yet in this, her proudest moment,
　　Her dread conscience battles still ;
With the gold from outer darkness,
　　Comes a wailing and a chill.

Turning, striving to the threshold—
　　Truth, and purity of heart ;
Her good angels from her girlhood
　　Weep and tremble, and depart.

Tint by tint with her attractions
　　Nature works, and wins her way :
Step by step with benefactions
　　Moves rich love on t'wards his prey.

Now the father is a farmer,
　　And full plenty round him sees :
And the mother in her dairy
　　Glories in her cream and cheese.

See ! their thymy upland pastures,
　　Spotted white with numerous sheep ;
And the meadow-grazing cattle,
　　'Mid the luscious grass knee-deep :

See! their pigeons cloud the dovecote,
    And the yard with poultry swarm :
See! the ruddy hanging fruitage,
    In the orchard of the farm.

See! along the walls and ceiling
    Where the lordly flitches swing,
Hams and bacon ; I'm mistaken
    If a farm is not the thing!

Often comes the landlord there—
    In his carriage there he drives ;
But the maiden feels despair
    When she thinks of happy wives.

For the rich man has a wife—
    Fond, devoted, true is she :
She who ponders in her hall,
    Whence his change of cheer may be.

But, erelong, she hears the rumour
    As she reads his altered eye :
And she feels herself a daisy
    When the rose is flaunting by.

But no word of jealous anger
    Aught of inward pangs disclose :
For the ancient farming people,
    Deep for them her pity flows.

Blinded by their better fortune,
　Strange it is they never think
That their daughter's degradation
　Is their daily meat and drink.

Or that cottage and its labour,
　With old fretting cares were sweet:
And the farm, with its abundance,
　Would be spurned with honest feet:

Would be spurned with indignation—
　For they lead a virtuous life;
Have for half a century prized it,
　Nearly so as man and wife.

And have seen their elder children
　Linked in wedlock's honest bands:
And have felt existence sweetened
　By the toil of virtuous hands.

Strange it is their daughter's ailments
　In them no suspicions wake:
Nor those sometimes far-off journeys
　Health compels that she should take.

Where, in fancied close seclusion,
　She gives birth unto a boy
Then—is of a girl the mother,
　But without a mother's joy.

Whence returning, paler, sadder,
    Of that life she feels the curse,
As with void and yearning bosom
    She resigns them to the nurse.

Oft, how sinks her heart with sadness!
    As in its plain drapery drest,
Her poor virtuous sister's baby
    Nestles in her conscious breast.

Yet, again upon the farm
    Soon the amorous web she weaves;
Stealthily upon the farm,
    Her rich lover she receives.

Still there is, however wary,
    Much they cannot wholly hide;
Whilst of those secreted children
    Flies the whispered rumour wide.

But the years keep onward speeding,
    And as strong the children grow,
Downward feeble, ever feebler,
    Graveward the old people go.

Onward speed the years, still onward!
    Who may time's stern march arrest?
And her Parents, not untroubled,
    Find a graveyard pillow best.

For no thorns are in that pillow,
　But with lethe-balm is blest:
Where the slanderers cease to slander,
　And the slandered are at rest.

Onward speed the years! still onward!
　And the lady of the hall
Has exchanged her living sorrow
　For the winding sheet and pall.

Round their dead adorèd mistress,
　Reverently her servants stand,
Whilst the old and shrivelled sinner
　On the coffin lays his hand.

In his mind there is commotion;
　Bitterness of inward strife;
For he knows, and no one better,
　She deserved a happier life.

Childless in her home, and lonely—
　Mother of the pained and poor;
Midst the sorrows of the many
　She is borne forth from her door.

Lonely also at the farm-stead
　Is that unwed mother there,
But now come her alien children,
　Brought to prove a mother's care.'

Reft from one to them the dearest,
 Whose adopted name they bear;
Brought to one for whom they care not,
 Wrung with anguish and despair.

Mother! as such will she own them,
 She who has not been a wife?
No—she never can relinquish
 Outside decencies of life.

These connections disconnected,
 All are of one wretched piece!
And that boy she calls her nephew—
 And her daughter is—her niece!

Of the church a strict frequenter,
 Most religious in her pew,
Of good worldly, moral people
 Are her visitors not few.

Gentry, clergy—both receive her,
 Enter too her gates within,
Who would scorn her, and would leave her,
 Did she own her well-known sin.

Comes no more the lover-landlord;
 Wrought his lady's death such change?
For no more his ancient favourite
 Seeks he at the lonely grange.

There the curate, from a distance,
   On the sabbath stays to dine:
And with that unwedded mother,
   Sits, and sips the racy wine.

Heavens! how hardly people judge her!
   Is she bad as these suppose,
Who from earthly peace would cast her,
   And heaven's gates against her close?

Happier, poorest wife and mother!
   Who no flagrant life conceals;
With hard cares—but consolations
   The aunt-mother never feels!

1852.

THE SLEEP OF THE YEAR.

Now frolicksome fruit-bearing Nature is dull,
'Tis the sleep of the year, for its garners are full:
When if for a moment we linger or roam,
The fields are forlorn, and we hie away home.
The hearty old farmer now fills up his glass,
Fills his pipe, too, that time may more cozily pass:
His tastes never costly, yet unto him dear,
He lives at his ease in the sleep of the year.

His fields, deeply ploughed, are prepar'd for the frost,
That all things may serve him, and nothing be lost:
Well drained and well furrowed: he's quite at his ease,
And rains may fall heavy, or not, as they please.
His cattle look well, deeply bedded in straw,
Well housed and well fed, now the weather is raw.
His barns all brimfull, his stackyard, too, near,
A solid affair in the sleep of the year!

His farm is his garden, you see 'tis his pride,
For neatness, for produce known both far and wide:
And of sheep, and of cattle, well bred, he can speak:
And see but his horses—how strong and how sleek!

His face and his fire well each other beseem,
Whilst he breathes out the smoke in a leisurely stream.
You see what he thinks of—his face makes it clear—
His harvest is made, 'tis the sleep of the year!

The peer, or the statesman—what cares he for them?
Or prince in his palace—for root or for stem?
His farm is his kingdom—he knows all is right;
He hears the flail going from morning till night.
His neighbours drop in, just to chat and to smoke;
To feel he is happy, and laugh at his joke:
His home is his palace—he's nothing to fear—.
But sinks to sweet sleep in the sleep of the year.

DEAD MEN'S SHOES.

"Riches make themselves wings."

Near to a shrubberied villa sat
A languid wight who gazed thereat:
Said I, "Whose dingy dome is that?"

"My kinsman's," gravely answered he,
"Who has no heir save him you see—
I pine—he's rich—and ninety-three."

Softly to him I made reply—
"For dead men's shoes who idly sigh,
Find out, that such men never die."

By mocking fortune 'tis adjusted,
Thus sportsmen, who for game have trusted,
Find feathers—where the birds have dusted.

FACTORY HONEY-DEW.

KEEN hawk, on that old elm-bough gravely sitting,
  Tearing that singing-bird with desperate skill;
Great nature says that what thou dost is fitting,—
  Through instinct, and for hunger, thou dost kill.

Rend thou the yet warm flesh, 'tis thy vocation;
  Mind thou hast none—nor dost thou torture *mind;*
Nay, thou, no doubt, art gentle in thy station,
  And, where thou killest, art most promptly kind!

On other tribes the lightning of thy pinion
  Flashing descends, nor always on the weak:
In other hawks, the mates of thy dominion,
  Thou dost not flesh thy talons and thy beak.

O, natural hawk, our lords of wheels and spindles,
  Gorge as it grows the liver of their kind:
Once in their clutch both mind and body dwindles:
  For gain to mercy is both deaf and blind.

O, instinct there is none—nor show of reason,
  But outrage gross on God and nature's plan,
With rarest gifts in blasphemy and treason,
  That man, the souled, should piecemeal murder man.

1847.

ANNE BOLEYN'S EXECUTION.

The Nero of England was silent and stern,
    His morning repast was a sombre affair;
Whilst they who his lightest wishes would learn,
    Lingered apart in tremor and care .

They knew that Anne Boleyn was doomed to the block,
    Who wrote bitter truths to the tyrant in power;
They saw that he listened to start at the shock
    Of the cannon, the signal, that boomed from the
      Tower.

"Hah! it is done!" the dread tyrant cried—
    "Uncouple the dogs, and let us to horse."
For he knew that his high-minded, once-favoured bride,
    By the axe and the block lay a weltering corse.

"Away!" for he fain the reflection would drown—
    In the stir of the chase would remember no more,
The beautiful head he had graced with a crown,—
    The neck he had folded, now streaming with gore.

TO A REDBREAST SINGING IN AUGUST.

Oh! Redbreast, why that early trill?
  The very leaves will feel alarmed,
And at that strain so autumn-chill,
  Will be of summer strength disarmed.

Nay, from this hoary apple-tree,
  Large yellow leaves fall to the ground,
As, Robin Redbreast! stirred by thee,
  They sympathise with that old sound.

These mists which on the morning hang,
  Awake such notes before their time,
For even now the cuckoo sang,
  A bird that loves no chilly clime.

Then, Robin, cease awhile that song,
  Till swallows thick of flight confer,
Nor do September grievous wrong,
  As it the month of August were.

I love thy song, but sing not now,
  Lest all the birds of summer rise,
From heath and meadow, dome, and bough,
  And plume their wings for southern skies.

The glow-worm yet is on the grass,
　　The leaves, tho' dark, as yet are green;
The flowers—not all yet from us pass,
　　But even now it Spring has been.

It seems but yesterday that we
　　Were gazing on pale primrose flowers,
On greening field, on leafing tree;
　　And thou dost hail autumnal hours!

O, sing not yet! but let the leaves
　　Grow russet with a slow decay;
For yet its nest the skylark weaves,
　　And sings—It is a summer's day.

Robin! the autumn all is thine,
　　'Midst falling leaves to pipe thy fill:
And it *will* come, with sure decline;
　　Then cease, and 'twill be summer still.

Summer supreme! matured from spring,
　　More matron-like in grace and worth,
Of heavenlier mould, a holier thing
　　As God and angels homed on earth!

1847.

CHRIST'S MISSION.'

For what came Christ on earth to reign;
   What aim had his love-labour?
It was that self-love might be slain,
   That man might love his neighbour.

Or, that every parish priest,
   Might have a lordly living?
If so, then each learned clerk
   Need feel no dread misgiving.

Came Christ to hallow swords and spears,
   For slaughter men like cattle?
Then, indeed the best renown
   Were only earned in battle.

Patience, fortitude, and faith,
   Evil with good requited,
Are victories on a bloodless field,
   Whose heroes are not knighted.

"My kingdom is not of this world!"
   O, soul of Julius Cæsar!
For all with conquering flags unfurled,
   That sentence is a teazer.

And not alone for martial pests,—
　For all earth's cunning brothers,
Who, not with their own shares content,
　Are daily robbing others.

The blood and tears of toil are shed,
　And slavery's groans are uttered,
That dainty rogues may have their bread
　On both sides nicely buttered.

Christ came not on the earth for this:—
　He will'd wrongs should be righted;
Not that the probed and trampled heart
　Should evermore be slighted.

"All are," said Christ, "the sons of God—
　The low are high in merit;
The meek are heritors of earth,
　And rich the poor in spirit."

Luxurious greatness! climb your towers
　And pinnacles of glory:
Thence see all kingdoms of the world,
　Like Christ, and read their story.

'Tis of vast multitudes athirst,
　Some better state pursuing—
(Such followed Christ)—whom ever ye,
　Lead on to their undoing.

With light from Heaven ye should them cheer,
  With goodness thence should cherish:
Yet these in time's dread wilderness,
  Lie daily down, and perish.

Read more—see luxury famine-dragged,
  Where ruin comes not single;
But rich and poor, the prince and boor,
  In one dread carnage mingle.

Again shall "evil be our good?"
  Is desolation wanted?
Again must murder be enthroned,
  Be-laurelled, and be-chanted?

Down with the tyrant Ignorance!
  On Pride the oppressor, trample!
That man with man may nobly plan,
  And good as life be ample.

O, TO BE YOUNG!

O, TO be young! whilst good is growing,
And life is some new wonder showing;
Whilst mind expands, and art advances,
And time at new discovery glances.   ·
David, inspired, in song had merit:
Homer was blest in his own spirit;
But Milton was the happier being,—
His works by them unseen, theirs seeing.

O, brave new world! Columbus sought thee,
But what thou art had he forethought thee,
The vision large his soul possessing,
His heart had burst with too much blessing.
The Austral world—through talk unstable,
In Cowper's day appeared a fable,
Yet there, through foam, the steamer rages,
And routs the ocean sleep of ages.

And on we press—to life before us,
And watch the dawn that brightens o'er us;
Mid knowledge vast of time's discovering;
And other near us largely hovering.

O, to be young! we seem but newly
Come on the earth, nor know her truly:
Whilst memory yearly grows more wealthy:
And hope more vigorous is, and healthy:
As interest grows in human doings,
Midst hope's designs, and memory's ruins,
Age on us steals, with death, presuming,
And blanks for us the ages coming.

O, to be young! still happier mortals,
Sons of the dawn, now burst its portals:
Born where the light is stronger, bolder,
Whilst we are waning dimmer, older.
Upon our dust come these to trample,
Of soul ethereal, mould more ample.

O, to be young! whilst good is growing,
And time is some new wonder showing:
Now the old darkness fast is waning;
And wide and wider Christ is reigning.
Peace is a glorious chief! Creation
Fast hastens to its renovation:
Where man, new-born in love's endeavour—
Heaven and the earth are one for ever!

1846.

THE MAN THAT BRINGS THE MONEY IN.

A WIFE'S LYRIC.

I DO my best to crown his days
With gladness, whom all love, or praise:
Whose early looks were sad and thin,
The man that brings the money in.

Through pain, through poverty, he wrought,
With skill of hand, and force of thought;
And made his way, despite his kin,
The man that brings the money in.

And wedded life, by many feared,
For him life's onward path has cleared:
Help, counsel he knew where to win,
The man that brings the money in.

He is the best good man alive,
And knows the best sure way to thrive:
All waste of time he counts a sin,
The man that brings the money in.

All tavern signs, old boars and bears—
To which the swinish man repairs,—
He scorns their lures of ale and gin—
The man that brings the money in.

He thinks for us the live-long year,
And toils, and thus is doubly dear:
And better days to dawn begin,
For him who brings the money in.

With love our humble home o'erflows—
It streaks the dawn, it tints the close.
And chucking many a rosy chin,
He laughs who brings the money in.

O! joy for us when evening falls,
And firelight dances round the walls:
When youngsters hail with merry din,
The man that brings the money in.

A VILLAGE INCIDENT.

WHY throng the people to this place,
    The churchyard of a village small;
Each with a sad and thoughtful face—
    From pity in the hearts of all?

I see it is the closing scene
    Of one, whose life had long been doomed:
Ah! better had she never been—
    Who here is brought to be entombed.

Outraged from this still spot she fled,
    To die 'mid London's ceaseless stir:
And now, from her afflictions dread,
    How meet this rest appears for her.

This vale long knew her, this still vale—
    As maiden, mother, and as wife;
But never heard it sadder tale,
    Than this, of her unhappy life.

Through suffering we are all allied—
    And here it is that death is best:
Death grants her what the world denied—
    Pardon, and pity, praise, and rest.

She who on every hand had blame,—
  Now "felt for others in distress:
And when her sister died became,
  True mother to the motherless."

But, see! the corse comes to the grave,—
  As from the heaving ocean's breast,
Rolls to the shore a weary wave,
  And sinks, and settles there to rest.

Around, above, the leafless sprays
  Tell of a resurrection bright:
Of life renewed in golden days,
  And wintry darkness lost in light.

Whilst solemnly the pastor's tones,
  Fall on the group far round him spread:
With hopes that dower the coffined bones,
  And bless and beautify the dead.

So young—so pitied—there she lies!
  But, shame to him who is not here;
Who would disgrace these obsequies—
  Yet should be foremost as most near.

I would not have his feelings now—
  The father of her only child,—
His memory how he kept his vow—
  For wealth up high as mountains piled.

Now all, who see her home—the place
  Where her few wretched years were passed,
Will there her wedded wrongs retrace,
  And all her sufferings to the last.

How by a brutal hand thrust down,
  As low as woman low can sink,
She sought her jealous woe to drown,
  In fatal, though oblivious drink.

Else she had sought that other door
  To Lethe and its shadows dark ;
Where the heart-fever burns no more—
  Extinction of life's vital spark.

And late she sought it,—but was met
  By one who cried, " Repent and pray ;
There is for thee acceptance yet !"
  And showed to her the better way.

For she, from home and hope exiled,
  Stript, smitten, forced by night to flee,
Had left, perforce, her only child,
  Whom never more she was to see.

. Fled vainly :—soon back hither cast,
  Thus prematurely to the grave.
So better, than the life she passed,
  Love's daily dying martyr-slave.

Peace, hence with that good sister go!
　Whose breast sustained the dying head:
Who tasked her utmost means to show
　This great respect unto the dead.

Who tasked her utmost means to keep
　Faith with the dying lips, that prayed
Here to be brought, and here to sleep,
　Near where a sister's dust is laid.

But he, who has the law escaped,
　Shall heavier penance undergo;
Who for his luckless victim shaped,
　Permitted murder—that is slow.

Remorse shall wake, and guilty fear!
　And guilt-imagined shapes draw nigh:
And he, as once before, shall hear,
　And see, what daunts no other eye!

Avenger-conscience! on thy wheel
　Rack him, who would not spare or save:—
Until he inly bleeds to feel,
　What sunk this woman to her grave!

January 1st, 1853.

7

ON THE DEATH OF AN ANCIENT VILLAGE LADY.

Her prized, smooth, ivory-headed cane,
May in its corner now remain :
Her chair be vacant, and the floor
Respond unto her foot no more.

How neatly mown her garden plot ;
Her flowers how fair now she is not :
The stonecrop on her porch how bright,
Now she no more enjoys the sight.

The priest will turn, and pause, and sigh,
As to the church he wanders by :
Will mark her grave beyond the yew :
And see with pain her vacant pew.

Her faults were by her neighbours shown ;
Her virtues only seemed unknown :
The first were buzzed amongst the crowd :
But now the last are all allowed.

We darkly move : we come and go :
Nor know ourselves, nor others know :
And what we are, and are to be,
Alone God's eye of love can see !

THE OLD SURPLICE.

"It hath been always true to the wear,
We've had it four and forty year."—OLD BALLAD.

It seems, when in my boyish days,
  The surplice on the priest I saw,
There mingled with that boyish gaze,
  A childish and mysterious awe.

It might have been by angels wrought,
  A holy garment from the sky:
But soon rush'd in the vulgar thought,
  'Twas made on earth for pomp to buy.

Thus dewdrops which like diamonds shine,
  Shook, fall to earth as dullest rain:
And fairy-frost-work, wondrous fine,
  Leaves on the glass a watery stain.

Flock after flock the dead are gone,
  Who listened to the sabbath text;
And formal Reverends, many a one,
  Have left the surplice to the next.

Some higher church preferment found,
  Where better preaching-price was given:
And some are laid low in the ground,
  To rise, so let us hope, in heaven.

Priest after priest departed hence—
   Yet priest we ne'er were known to lack :
Came he for practice, or for pence,
   The same good surplice graced his back.

One tipsy comes to meet the bier,
   Who buries a poor mason's wife :
What is't he says? pray let us hear—
   " The Resurrection and the Life !"

He! dead in trespasses and sins—
   The dead, who buries there the dead !
At whom the knowing Atheist grins,
   And good men troubled hang the head.

Another locks the churchyard gate ;
   And claims the sward where sheep are fed :
That vainly mourners come and wait,
   By that new prison of the dead.

The learned priest, the parson dull ;
   The lean and the plethoric stout ;
All fill'd the allotted time up full—
   And yet the surplice wore not out.

And once it made a glorious show,
   That warm'd men through their utmost veins ;
When of a good man's face the glow
   It caught, like light from heavenly plains.

It oftener seemed a tinsel skin,
  Slough of the Serpent of the Fall:
The borrowed angel-robe of sin—
  Or merest piece of whited wall.

And now there swells a general cry,—
  The holy rag is past repair;
And that we must a surplice buy,
  Fit for our dapper priest to wear.

And churchrates—earnings of the poor—
  Must on this wretched mission fly:
And they, the poor, as heretofore,
  Be paid with dead-leaf sermons dry.

Christ's little flock, that should be fed,
  By shepherds of a watchful eye,
Are famished, O, the feeling dread!
  And in their destitution die!

But, here a moment let us stop,
  This priestly custom, is it fair?
We find him wages, and a shop,
  And keep his workshop in repair:

And shall he wear a parish dress,
  As paupers do?   It should not be:
Time couches nations, more or less,
  For blindness—yet men will not see!

GOOD DEEDS SELF-REWARDING.

" Our neighbour's gate," an old man said,
All anxiously upon his bed,
" Stood open wide, yet when I pass'd,
At eve I did not make it fast.

" Some evil, or some careless folk,
So left it," he continuing spoke:
" And all his cattle, ere the morn,
Will revel in his standing corn.

" How could I pass it thus, and see?
And yet the thing concerns not me:
The man is absent, but his men,
Should stop all mischief there and then.

" And so they might, and all be well:
I trust 'tis so, but cannot tell:
I trust—and yet that corn is bread,
Wherewith the hungry must be fed.

" This autumn night the air is chill:
With hoar-frost white are dale and hill:
And night-air is a thing to dread:
And I am old, and warm in bed.

"And yet it were a grievous loss,
All that fine corn to Farmer Moss."
As thus the old man thought and said,
He sigh'd, and tumbled in his bed.

"Well, surely, sleep has left these eyes,—"
The old man groan'd, "I e'en must rise."
For, in despite of age and frost,
He felt the corn should not be lost.

"I e'en must rise, let what will come:
That crop is worth a serious sum:
Yet, pause a moment, let me see,
Would surly Moss do so by me?

"Did he not pound my sheep—and fell
The tree so prized above our well—
And stopp'd the village road? The man
Still does what worthless mortal can."

Uprising, to the gate he went,
Safe made it, and returned content:
Return'd content, and somewhat more—
And slept, where slept he not before.

Thenceforth, when came that deed to mind,
It left a pleasant sense behind:
As violets which have long been dead,
Surviving sweetness round them shed.

Hood's Mag. 1845.

THE HEANOR CHURCHYARD YEW.

ADDRESSED TO EVA.

O! Eva, daughter of old Eve!
What! would you have a bard believe,
That not yet unto death was due,
That battered, ugly, churchyard yew!

Some geni whispers, what is strange!
That in this world of ceaseless change,
'Mid life and death, 'mid smiles and tears,
That tree has stood a thousand years!

"What! older than the church?" you cry—
"Yes! older than the church," say I:
"For, centuries ere that church arose,
There stood the chapel, all suppose.

"And in that graveyard the remains
Were laid of Saxons, Normans, Danes:
Where first, in glossy youth, up-grew—
Our sable friend, the reverend yew.

"The oak five centuries will grow:
Five more will little difference shew:
And other five will wear away,
In imperceptible decay!

"The yew will twice that term endure!
An axe is then its only cure:
Hew it, and root it from its bed—
Defying death amongst the dead!

" 'Tis gone! good riddance! let it go—
That the next century may show,
Instead, with branches waving free,
A beautiful, umbrageous tree!

"From the far centuries, hoar, and dim,
The yew exists, hard, gaunt, and prim:
As though, in scorn of our brief span,
Lasting, and lording it o'er man.

" 'Man's life is threescore years and ten:'
'A woman's is—the Lord knows when!'*
Therefore, fair Eva! bear in mind,
The yew is tough as womankind!

"I joke—yet not the less I know,
How much we unto woman owe,
As mother, daughter, sister, wife,
Gracing, and blessing, human life.

* Dr. Johnson.

" The yew a symbol is—a sign,
Of life more lasting and divine.
Hint, intimation sent from far,
Beyond the farthest, faintest star.

" Will He, who gives the yew such strength—
And years of such protracted length,
Give, Eva! unto you and me,
Less life than to a soulless tree?"

HARVESTS OF TIME.

MANKIND have something wrought ere this,
　Around, within us, and beneath:
And we our mission use amiss,
　If nothing added we bequeath.

The wind which seems to blow to waste,
　Even it on man vast wealth confers:
Impelling ships with wingèd haste—
　And giving strength to what it stirs.

It plants more firm the mountain pine—
　It makes more strong the giant oak ;—
An idler in the poet's line,—
　Man has subdued it to his yoke.

He has subdued the fire, the flood—
　Brute matter owns his sovereign sway :
And mighty energies, for good,
　A mightier energy obey.

Else ours had been the primal lot,
    Through man's omissions, or his sins;
The primal fate, deserved or not,
    To eat raw beasts, and wear their skins.

Mankind have something wrought ere this—
    And products of the soul and sod,
Give man some cause to deem he is,
    Impulse of heaven through breath of God!

The old give place to newer grace—
    Art, science, gain us more and more;
And mind with time keeps equal pace,
    For wants no age has waked before.

The years have sown what years shall reap,
    An ample, and yet ampler yield.
The victors of the world, who sleep,
    Left spoils on many a bloodless field!

Mankind have something wrought ere this!
    To higher life, progressing yet!
As from the past great largess is,
    The future claims as large a debt.

Make way for good, whate'er it be,
    And whencesoever it may come,
That we yet added wealth may see,
    In mien and mind, in heart and home!

DREAM-FRAGMENT.

I STOOD before the threshold of a cave—
A natural temple of the unhewn stone
High-overarched and ruggedly sublime.
The lion at the entrance slept. Within
Were hoary fathers of the antient world,
Sages and poets, prophets and old kings.
Milton, with Homer walking, talked apart:
Alfred with David, Socrates with Christ.
Far in broad vistas from me stretched the land:
Fair land that seemed, most meet for pastoral folk.

On trees of giant bole, and shadowy breadth,
Wondering I gazed. Soft lapsing streams were heard.
That over gems, and golden sands sang on,
'Twixt emerald banks, delicious with all flowers.
Light—whence it came I knew not—light with
        shade
Alternate, evermore refreshed the sight;
For sun, or moon, or stars, were nowhere seen.
At intervals arose a freshening breeze,
A living impulse, as it seemed, intense—

That shook the woods, and all as sudden leapt
The birds to song, and as it ended, ceased.
Joy was a living presence—Silence sweet
After glad sound: on every hand was joy.
Then said I to myself—"Time is no more—
Life into nobler being has ascended—
And is no longer heavy earthly life."

A MORAL OF THE IVY AND THE OAK.

The ivy grew strong, the ivy grew bold,
And clasped the old oak round with many a fold:
It praised the old tree for a forester good,
The lord of nature, and grace of the wood.
The ivy grew fat, seemed loving and meek,
And graced the rough oak with a mantle sleek;
Whilst, day after day, and year after year,
The oak looked around with a lusty cheer;
The jolly old oak, the playmate of Time,
That many a year had thus stood in his prime.
The ivy, a thing but of yesterday's growth,
Seemed of such fellowship not to be loth,
But shot out his fibres, and spread forth his shoots—
And deeper and faster struck downward his roots:
He bit through the bark, and made sure of the wealth—
And smiled at his progress, and masterly stealth;
And quaffed of the oak's blood many a health.
The oak was a giant, and what should he care
That the ivy should get of his heart's blood a share?
No niggard was he—no—it gave him delight
When the ivy swelled large as the son of his might.

But the oak had of acorns before-time increase,
And sons he had nurtured mid plenty in peace :
Yet the soil that the acorns were dropped in was bad,
And regard to the shade of the Parent was had :
Whilst the ivy, the Parasite, looked somewhat blue,
And said, " I am his—will he succour these too ?
I'm the stay of his age—I adorn his old pate—
My own wants are urgent—the others must wait."
Now the oak, the good oak, had quite lived out his
          term :
The axe he had missed, but old age has its worm :
So down with the earth he was levelled at last,
And the sons which he sheltered lay bare to the blast.
But what of the ivy ?   'Twas shaken, but grew,
And unto itself said, " 1 think I shall do,—
I held the old oak up 1 think I may say—
Might fancy too often he stood in my way—
I've gotten much good,—but alas, but alas,
For the sap,—I am not so well off as I was."
He tried at a smile—in his heart there was grief,
For he knew all the world would now term him a thief.
From his front the full rose of assurance was plucked,
With the death of the giant whose blood he had sucked.
He sighed, " When the storms rise, oh, where shall I
          be ?
Alas ! for the bonny old burly oak tree !"
The sons of the oak, now dissatisfied more,
Well knowing the ivy had wronged them before,

Cried out with one voice—" For the day, and the hour,
Thou grew'st with the oak, and wast firm as a tower:
But now, for his sap which thou hast in thy veins,
Of old, and for ever this justice remains,
The conscious injustice shall burn in thy blood—
For ill-gotten riches do nobody good!"

1819

IN MEMORIAM.

LINES

On reading the following obituary notice in a local newspaper—
"Died, at Shelton Rectory, on the 31st of December, 1858, the
Rev. Chas. Langley Maltby, in his 42nd year.

ARE these few bare words the only token
    Of him we see not, but fain would see:
Whose fire-touched lips have fervently spoken
    Of what Time is, and the Future will be;

Who lovingly followed his Master Holy,
    With christian charity, duty, and zeal—
Who ministered unto the poor and lowly,
    And, feeling himself, taught others to feel?

Remorse shall yet wake for one so forgiving,
    For one so generous, one so true:
Remorse shall yet wake in his enemies living,
    Who knew not the worth of him they slew.

O, clerical judge, who sate to try him,
    Turn back your eyes on the spots within;
For what you impute, or what you deny him,
    Be sure that yours is no graver sin.

Impurity never fell from his lips :
  Of hatred or slander he blew not the coals ;
Nor was he like many, a dread eclipse
  Betwixt the Almighty and human souls.

O, Church ! in whose temple he ministered duly,
  O, favoured Church ! of a famous land ;
God send forth thousands as worthily, truly,
  And purely as he at thine altars to stand.

O, Flock ! who had hailed with joy his returning,
  From clouds, which obscured, had he worked himself
    clear—
His darkened departure has left you in mourning,
  But long to your hearts will his memory be dear.

The keenest edge of the slander that slew him,
  In his manly worth, in his spirit's bloom,
With the loving regrets of the many who knew him,
  Attended him down to the silent tomb.

A VILLAGE LYRIC.

Our home is in a pleasant place,
Retired, yet rich in rural grace;
So near a Minster that ofttimes
We hear its clock and sweet old chimes.

A vale of smooth ascending land,
With nothing striking, nothing grand;
Yet where the eye, that roves in quest
Of beauty, still delights to rest.

O'er-azured with a hazy grace,
A slumbrous veil half folds the place:
A place endowed with endless charms
Of homesteads, cottages and farms.

Luxurious pride here seldom flaunts,
Or wretchedness of squalid haunts;
And blessed does the region seem
Alike exempt from each extreme.

In orchard-plots embosomed deep,
Sweet roses through bright windows peep,
Where love domestic dwells inshrined
In hearts intelligent and kind.

In spring, a pure delicious sight,
With plots of bloom the scene is white;
In May a rosy splendour fills
The vale, and spreading clothes the hills:

Rich orchard-bloom, whose fruits we prize,
Nor sigh for tropic fruits or skies;
Where gorgeous birds are harsh or mute,
And slavery groans 'midst golden fruit.

A higher moral tone pervades,
And kindlier virtues bless these shades :
Where, though more cold these northern parts,
Sincerer beat the manlier hearts.

Thus, in this vale retired, we know
What makes the British bosom glow :
And share, with mountain, and with sea,
The clime and soul that make us free.

THE DIFFERENCE.

The rich man for his doctor sends,
And round him press assiduous friends ;
Each face is drest in solemn pall,
And servants bustle in his hall.
The region into gloom is cast,
And messages fly far and fast ;
The proud world zealous all it can
To honour so august a man.
The fingered pulse—the shaken head—
The haunted door—the tended bed—
The stealthy pace, and constant light
Make known the rich man's wretched plight.
But worldly wealth, and wealth of kin,
Bring hourly store of solace in ;
And every want, and wish, and sigh,
Meets still a sympathetic eye.
Alternate are the hopes and fears
As danger fades, or reappears :
Till Physic from his bitter den
Routs Death, and in the walks of men
The Golden-calf has knees again ;
A worship old.   But where is he,

The man of pathos, wit, and glee:
Whose soul to highest heaven was caught
In glorious extasies of thought:
Large-hearted he, who longed to make
Life better for his fellows' sake:
Who shunned all contact mean and vile,
And the world shrunk from him the while,
The honourable man and poor?
In illness none besiege his door;
But quiet latch, and lonely room,
Declare his melancholy doom.
Of all his wealth of heart bereft—
Wife, children—he alone is left!
No wreck, a speck amid the sea,
Is more austerely left than he.
The eye of fire is grey and tame—
Depressed the heaven-erected frame:
Subdued the manly breadth of brow;
Who knew him—would they know him now?
Sorrowing and sickly, pained and poor—
Life and its means alike unsure:
He moves a shadow through still lanes,
That heard his keen or genial strains;
Unknown, unnoticed in his grief,
To fall like autumn's trembling leaf!

1851.

TROPICAL NIGHT THOUGHTS.

Written at Sea, latitude 7, North, longitude 24, West.

NIGHT broods over the ocean wide!
The waters heave, and ripple, and glide:
The air is so soft, that we scarcely know
Whether we sleep on the brine, or go.
The lightning slips from cloud to cloud,
But thunder is none, or low, or loud.
The crescent moon, a silver canoe,
Floats level through the rifts of blue,
Then cuts through a cloud and smiles anew.
The stars in heaven burn and glow,
Whilst this we feel, and this we know—
There's a God above, and his love below:
That thousands of voyagers there be
Who lie down to sleep on the mighty sea—
Putting their trust in God as we.

We have left the safe and the solid earth,
The home and the country of our birth;
The friends of our youth and our manhood's prime,
With thoughts of the past and the coming time.

Nor is it for lust of lucre alone
That we are over the waters blown :
That we from the land of our love are sped :
The land of our living, the land of our dead :
Our household gods have absolved us, to go,
More of the wondrous world to know :
Perchance that upon a foreign shore,
Loving our land we might love it the more.

Nor seem we away from our country and friends :
Or the love which everywhere extends.
Our dearest haunts we ever must see ;
With the most beloved we ever must be :
The love that was ours by an English fire-side ;
The affections over us still preside ;
They follow us over the ocean wide :
Like angels they start up from the past
And over us watch, and will to the last.

When vexed with calms, when tried with storms,
Their presence we feel though we see not their forms :
And of winds and of waves the sport, we come
To the same God, our haven and home!

Oct. 1839.

THE WELCOME VISITOR.

Written off the Cape Verd Isles

When weary, weary winter
  Had melted from the air,
And April leaf and blossom
  Had clothed the branches bare,
Came round our English dwelling
  A voice of summer cheer,
'Twas thine, returning swallow,
  The welcome and the dear.

We heard, amid the daybreak,
  Thy twitter blithe and sweet,
In life's auspicious morning,
  The precious and the fleet!
We saw thee lightly skimming
  O'er fields of summer flowers;
And heard thy song of inward bliss,
  Through evening's golden hours.

Far on the billowy ocean
  A thousand leagues are we,
Yet here, sad, hovering o'er our barque,
  What is it that we see?

Dear old familiar swallow!
What gladness dost thou bring!
Here rest upon our flying sail,
Thy weary, wandering wing.

What glimpses of our native homes,
And homesteads dost thou bring!
Here rest, upon our quivering mast,
Thy welcome, weary wing.
To see thee, and to hear thee
Amid the ocean's foam,
Again we see the loved, the left—
We feel at home—at home!

A SEA BALLAD.

He has shipped himself all on shipboard —
Some foreign land he would go see.
                    Old Ballad of Lord Bateman.

We had not been at sea, at sea,
   Weeks but barely three,
When our steward said, with a very long face,
   Not a bit of cheese had we.

The sago and the arrow-root
   Were done about the line:
And there were fears about the water,
   And doubts about the wine.

To eat the salt pork was sorry work—
   We boiled it both and fried;
The beef it was rank, and the water stank,
   And the pigs of the measles died.

We had not been at sea, at sea
   Weeks but barely five,
When every biscuit in the ship
   Began to be alive.

Some of them had been before
   A voyage in this same ship,
And so they grew rebellious,
   Not liking a second trip.

We stared on them you may be sure
   With looks of sore dismay,
For some were blue and some were green,
   And some were hoary grey.

They once were baked it was supposed,
   Although we couldn't tell when;
So, just to kill the living things,
   We baked them o'er again.

If Rutherford in his old age
   Should ask for parish relief,
God send he may eat his own biscuit,
   And try to eat his own beef.

We had not been at sea, at sea
   Weeks but barely six,
Before our tea was a black sea—
   Black as the river Styx.

At sea, at sea we had not been
   Weeks but barely seven,
When not a soul, of our company whole,
Thought biscuit was bread, or chalk was coal,
   Or that the sea was heaven!

We had not been, we had not been
   At sea weeks barely nine,
When the sea-carrion creatures
   Looked on and longed to dine.

The hungry shark, he sought our barque,
　And he was nothing coy,
He opened his mouth and wagged his tail
　As a dog might do for joy.

And, horrid thing! a mermaid sang—
　"I wonder how it floats—
This rotten ship upon the sea,
　With all its rotten boats." *

At this the sharks all clapped their fins,
　And leapt above the brine:
And showed again their readiness
　If they should come to dine.

Yet strange! our captain's full of glee,—
　He pokes our ribs in sport—
And says, "Come, comrades, port the helm,"
　And sits him down to port.

Alack, alack, I mickle fear—
　Though water has been scant—
We yet may have among our grog,
　More water than we want.

---

* A bullock put his foot through the bottom of the ship's long-
boat in Port Phillip Harbour, and the ship itself was condemned, the
next voyage, as unseaworthy.

AUSTRALIAN POEMS,

ETC.

SONNET.

WRITTEN WHEN "I TOO WAS AN ARCADIAN."

A CHEQUERED path through my own land I trod,
  Sad, yet with poesy flower-strewn to the last:
  That which has been may be not: o'er the past
The grave of distance closes like the sod.
For social life is savage, my abode
  The wilderness, the vacant and the vast.
  Yet grudge I not at fortune's gifts misplaced,
In my own soul confiding, and in God.
Here shall I bear the shepherd's crook—sage time
  And meditation my companions old:
Think much, read little, watch the heavens sublime,
  Like the Chaldeans nightly at the fold:
An exile—yet content in this bright clime—
  If I may gather golden thoughts and gold.

Melbourne, 1840.

TO THE DAISY.

ON FINDING ONE UNEXPECTEDLY IN AUSTRALIA, JULY
30TH, 1840.

WHENCE was the silvery gleam that came?
A daisy! can it be the same?
Some fairy from my native land,
For me this glad surprise has planned;
Of light and joy a sudden shower,
Or never had I seen this hour,
Our real English daisy-flower.

Daily I meet some shape or hue,
That brings old times before me new:
Some token of life's brightest hours,
In streams and trees, in birds and flowers:
The past is by such spells unbound:
But never, until now, have found,
What makes me feel on English ground.

Of poesy thou favourite child!
First seen when some blest angel smiled!
O'er Britain scattered everywhere—
But strangely solitary here:

Yet buoyant-looking, brisk, and bold,
That with like cheer do I behold,
Thy silver rays and disk of gold.

These mosses, ferns, resemble ours:
These sundew, sorrel, speedwell-flowers:
Yet none are in all points the same,
As in the isle from whence we came,
Save thee, dear daisy! thee alone—
Thy crimson tips proclaim thee known;
At once we hail thee all our own!

Now easy seems it to my mind,
I also may a primrose find
In some shy glen; or, it may be,
A cowslip nodding on the lea:
All things are possible, it seems,
To him, for whom the fairy schemes,
Whose waking hours are blest as dreams.

O, not miscalled the eye of day—
Sweet gowan of the Scottish brae!
Close shut at eve: with dawning light,
Opening on heathy summits bright:
When first the crimson streaks the gloom,
That very tint thou dost assume,
And sweetly blushest into bloom.

Flower of the dawn, and dawn of song!
O, well may grace to thee belong!

By ancient bards how blazoned wide—
And how by Wordsworth glorified!
And seen by Burns, he could not choose.
But crown thee with unfading hues—
Thou—lov'd of every sylvan muse!

In England thou art alway seen
On mead, on moor, on village-green:
In forest glen, on mountain height;
A common thing in common sight:
But here, 'mongst flowers superbly dressed,
Shalt thou, and prized o'er all the rest,
Become our cherished garden-guest.

Australian flowers I prize nor scorn:
Let those, who in this land were born,
Admire them, praise them, pluck, and wear,
On dusky brow, in jet-black hair:
I never gathered them, nor knew,
Where I a child to manhood grew;—
What have I then with them to do?

Yet flowers bloom here of loveliest dye,
Where roves and rests the enamoured eye;
Chaste forms, and tints of beauty rare:
For these no fondness can I spare;
Of song they have no generous dower;
No life-long memory, homely power,
Like thee, our darling English flower!

THE NATIVE WOMAN'S LAMENT.

WHEN he was weak, and we were strong,
　The white man's soul was warmth and light;
With friendly smiles and gentle tongue,
　He talked of reason and of right.

He asked of us in language meek,
　Where flocks and herds might well abide:
We led to river and to creek,
　Fair streams, and pastures green and wide.

He heard the river-bird content,
　Peal its sweet bells along the wave,
He by the Yarra pitched his tent,
　And to us food of wonder gave.

But now they rise on every hand,
　As clouds o'er heaven that move and spread;
They thrust our living from the land,
　And build their domes upon our dead.

" Gigo," the white man cries " away!"
　He points us, nor delays to push ;
" We have no food for you to-day—
　Away, black Lubra, to the bush."

Now they are many, we are few,
　　Still brightly shines the sun and moon:
The white man wears an altered hue,
　　His soul and face are dark at noon.

We wander o'er the weary plain,
　　But rarely meet the fleet emu:
We search for food the woods in vain
　　Nor ask who killed the kangaroo.

The white man wanders in the dark;
　　We hear his thunder smite the bough:
The opossum's mark upon the bark
　　We traced, but cannot find it now.

The white man tells us where to go;
　　He tells us where to turn and stand:
Where our old creeks and rivers flow,
　　In their old freedom through the land!

His flocks and herds our forests fill:
　　A thousand woods we wander through,
And hunger—yet we may not kill
　　The white man's woolly kangaroo.

O, sorrow! weary little one!
　　O, helpless and ill-fated child!
The food, the life, the land is gone—
　　And we must perish in the wild!

TO THE RIVER YARRA-YARRA.

CHILD of the hills—the forest child!
Unwearied wanderer of the wild:
Thou, Yarra, art a stream sincere,
As ever soothed the poet's ear.
Although by minstrel yet unsought—
Unsung—unknown in hallowed thought!
O, mirror of fair forms! thou source
Of joy along thy mazy course.

Not soon shall we forget how first,
On us thy primal beauty burst;
With trees of trunk and limb sublime,
As they had grown from oldest time:
Woods over woods, and hills far-seen,
With knolls, and slopes, and glens between;
Where Art had entered not—our way
Taking through endless forests grey:
Where all we met was new and rare,
And all we saw was good and fair.

But Yarra, thou art lovelier now,
With clouds of bloom on every bough:

A gladsome sight it is to see,
In blossom thy mimosa tree.
Like golden moonlight doth it seem,
The moonlight of a heavenly dream ;
A sunset lustre, chaste and cold,
A pearly splendour, blent with gold ;
That in its loveliness profound,
The waters have a mellower sound.

When Eve, fresh from the Almighty's hand
Moved graceful in the orient land,
And gladness, like a river, flowed
On with her through that blest abode ;
Light from her limbs diffused—a fine
Effulgence of the touch divine ;
Pure as an angel, and as fair,
Such blossom might she pluck and wear.

Free—waving wide, ascending high,
And to the waters drooping nigh,
There shows of myriad flowers a gleam,
Trembling in the glassy stream :
'Midst azure gleams a golden glow,
In the softer heavens below,
Blent with clouds of purest snow.
O, well may Yarra turn and stay,
Well may she here and thither stray ;

Oft turn, and fold herself to sleep,
As loth to join the oozy deep:
Even like a maiden blooming bright,
Who turns on home a lingering sight,
And for the first time, leaves in tears,
The home of love from earliest years.
In sooth the whole wide vale is fair—
And spicy rich the odorous air.

Flow on, sweet Yarra! time shall be,
Shall happy votaries crowd to thee;
And smiles of cultured beauty bless
With theirs, thy natural loveliness.
These miams soon will disappear,
Rude sheds which thy dark people rear;
Domes of a race uncouth, forlorn,
Wide-scattered by the winds of scorn.
Whate'er the good may do or say,
Self-moving to a sure decay,
Possessing nothing to retard,
Of slighted arts the sure award,
Thy ancient tribes will pass away.
Others now seek thy flowery bed:
Here social life will bloom instead;
And cottage hall, and rural farm,
Will rise to cheer thee, and to charm.
O, Yarra; worthy highest place!
No more wilt thou reflect a race
Squalid in form, in aspect base.

Fair girls from England's lovely land,
Bright as thy bloom will by thee stand;
And stooping low thy waves will kiss
Lips pure as from the realms of bliss ;
And in return wilt thou disclose,
Fair brows, clear seen in thy repose,
Our England's lily and its rose.

Joy to thee, Yarra! be thou blest!
The weary come to thee for rest.
Far England's care-worn sons and daughters,
Sad ocean-pilgrims, seek thy waters.
And some of those who to thee flock,
Are beings of earth's noblest stock ;
Heroic, just : who could endure
Great sorrows that they might be pure :
Who, in the land they left, resigned
Much—not the heaven-erected mind ;
Nor firmest will : nor native dower
Of moral, and creative power.
These with them bring their treasures old,
Stores of the soul, if not of gold ;
And added unto thee shall make
Thee, Yarra, famous for their sake.

The Tweed is now a wondrous river!
The Ayr flows on in song for ever!
The Cam and Isis have a fame,
With streams of Greek and Roman name.

And Thames, and Trent, and Ouse, shall charm,
Wherever song the heart can warm.
And, Yarra, a strong heart hast thou :
For honouring wreaths an ample brow :
And hence, in strains that will endure,
Will poets sing thee, Yarra pure.
And hence the manly and the fair,
Will pace thy borders free from care ;
And wine, and song, and lover's tale,
Will one Arcadia make thy vale.

Melbourne, 1840.

TULLAMARINE.

Tullamarine, thou lovely flower,
I saw thee in a happy hour:
When first I gazed upon my boy
I saw thee with a mother's joy.

Methought thy beauty on me smiled,
And by thy name I called my child:
And thence alike with joy were seen
Both boy and flower, Tullamarine.

The lights in heaven appear and go:
Both flowers and stars their seasons know;
Thus in thy season, thou art seen,
Sweet earthly star, Tullamarine.

Soother of many a weary hour,
By mountain stream, in forest bower:
I gathered thee with choicest care,
And wore thee fondly in my hair.

Wide wandering through the woods away,
Where with thy bloom the ground was gay,
I called thee then the " flower of joy,"
Sweet namesake of my darling boy.

He grew: he flourished by my side;
He ran, he gathered thee with pride:
But, woe is me! in evil hour
Death stole away my human flower.

I wander in my spirit's night,
My star is emptied of its light;
Thou, flower of joy, art changed to grief;
Thy dews, my tears are on thy leaf.

Therefore do I behold in vain
Thy beauty: look on it with pain;
I see thee with an inward groan,
Because I look on thee alone.

All things my sorrow seem to share:
There broods a sadness on the air;
There hangs a gloom along the sky,
My boy is dead and thou shouldst die.

Now for the joy which long I had,
The sight of thee must make me sad:
So in my path no more be seen,
But deck his grave, Tullamarine.

Tullamarine, a month or twain
Thy annual smiles must breed me pain :
But blunt for me thy sorrows keen,
Sweet flower of tears, Tullamarine.

NOTE.—I had the incident on which this simple ballad is founded
from a gentleman who had been a Church Missionary amongst the
natives.   How strange, these uncouth beings have, it would seem,
human, natural feelings—the instincts and passions of their kind.

OLD IMPRESSIONS.

Nay—tell me not, the exile said,
  You think this land as fair as ours,
That endless spring is round us spread ;
  That blessings rise on every hand :
O, give to me our country's flowers—
  And give to me our native land.

Our churchyard, with its old grey wall ;
  Our church with its sweet sabbath bell ;
Our village fields, so green and small ;
  The primrose in my native dell ;
I see, I hear, I feel them all—
  In memory know and love them well.

The bell-bird, by the river heard ;
  The whip-bird, which surprised I hear,
In me have powerful memories stirred
  Of other scenes and strains more dear.—
Of sweeter songs than these afford,
  The thrush and blackbird warbling clear.

The robin which I here behold
 Most beautiful with breast of flame!
No cottage-enterer shyly bold;
 No household bird in seasons drear;
Is wild, is silent: not the same
 Babe-burying bird of ancient fame:
Where is the strain I wont to hear,
 The song of russet leaves and sere?
O, call it by some other name!

I'm tired of woods for ever green:
 I pine to see the leaves decay:
To see them, as our own are seen,
 Turn crimson, orange, russet, grey:
To see them, as I've seen them oft,
By tempests torn and whirled aloft;
 Or, on some bland autumnal day,
A golden season still and soft,
In woodland walk, in garden croft,
 Die silently and drop away.

The fields in which my youth was spent,
The scenes through which I daily went;
 Went daily through and did not see,
On inward visions fair intent;
 Those scenes for which I had no eyes,
Where in the wild-thyme hummed the bee,
 I now have rightly learned to prize;
 To me in dreams do they arise—
With tenderest hues they visit me.

Then tell me not, the exile said,
  This land may not compare with ours,
Though endless spring be round us spread,
  Though blessings rise on every hand:
O, give to me our country's flowers—
  And give to me our native land.

But more than all, the exile said,
  In this poor country of a day,
Where rise the works of ages fled,
  Your halls and ivied castles grey ?
  Your ancient cities where are they ?
Where live your sculptors', painters' toil,
That consecrate the meanest soil ?
    Where, whither shall we turn to find
    Man's noblest monuments of mind ?

The spirit of this clime is tame ;
  The aspect of this race is cold:
To buy and sell their souls they frame ;
  The worship of the land is gold.
With these no sympathy may claim
Our ancient bards of mighty fame,
    Our statesmen, and our warriors old.

By no dull ties of custom bound
  In that sweet land which first I knew,
A world within a world I found
  And from this sordid life withdrew.

By soul-enlarging genius led
I traversed wide the realms of mind ;
And communed with the living dead,
The deathless sages of mankind.

From out decay the springing flowers
Rise hallowed in that northern clime :
O, what a place of birth was ours,
The land of Memory and of Time !

Australia, 1841.

TO THE DAISY,

On again finding one in Australia, Sept. 12, 1841.

Meets the miner casual treasure,
   Quick he looks for other store;
At this unexpected pleasure,
   Round me thus I search for more:
Yet, unlooked-for daisy, thou
Art my sole discovery now.

Years have passed since of thy kind
   One I in Australia saw;
And from that great joy of mind
   Often could I solace draw:
Hope with chance delights to meet,
Made by hallowing memories sweet.

Thou dost bring as from the dead
   Visions of our English lark,
Warbling blithely overhead:
   And the bird that cheers the dark:
In those seasons of delight
When thou wert in daily sight.

10

When a bowery village lane,
    Copse, or dell, or chiming brook,
Homely, well could entertain
    As an ever-open book;
Fancy, feeling, thoughts which grew
Hourly, fed with wonders new.

All an exile's sadness seems
    Round thee lonely flower to brood:
As if food of far-off dreams
    Sole sustained this solitude:
As a nature far apart
From home-happiness and heart.

Heart reliance can be none
    Where no life-long mate is seen
Of the many left not one.
    Gems of sward like emeralds green,
Waked by spring's benign regard,
Merry masquers of the sward!

Were this little alien flower,
    That so near thee neighbouring dwells,
Our own cowslip, hour by hour,
    From its pendant odorous cells
What old greetings would there run
To thee in the breeze and sun.

Still its aspect brightens thine,
   For resemblance it displays
To our little Celandine,
   Golden star with gorgeous rays;
Whilst this violet pink and blue,
Seems an old friend in a new.

Hence despond not—let us cherish
   Offered heart's-food far or nigh :
What is garnered will not perish
   Whilst the " worship of a sigh"
Pays the spirit to life's prime ;
Scenes and seasons yoked with time.

ALIEN SONG.

BLIND Homer sung in alien realms
    Heroic strains of deeds sublime :
Thus he whom absence overwhelms
    May sing for every land and time.

With Gama went the Lusian bard,
    First Eastern India to explore ;
He sung, and now has his reward,
    Contemned, neglected now no more.

Tasso, immersed in dungeon glooms
    From friends and home scenes pined apart :
Yet still in vigorous beauty blooms
    The amaranth of the poet's heart.

The bird that nightly carols sweetest
    An alien is in British bowers :
The first to come, to go the fleetest,
    And sings to cheer the darksome hours.

By alien streams sad Hebrew sages
    Their harps had fain on willows hung,
Yet vibrate still through latest ages
    The mournful numbers which they sung.

In fields as Bethel bright or Haran,
  Carmel or Seir my being grew:
'Midst flowers sweet as the rose of Sharon,
  Or lilies wet with Hermon's dew.

Where woman's warmth and light are heaven,
  'Midst noblest shapes of manly mind;
To me a life enlarged was given
  And earth's dull nature half divined.

For this 'midst Austral wilds I waken
  Our British harp, feel whence I come,
Queen of the sea, too long forsaken,
  Queen of the soul, my spirit's home!

SONNET.

THEMES for Australian poets loveliest flowers
Fix sweet regards upon me: some with eye
Serious and thoughtful; others archly sly.
Amongst them do I spend delightful hours,
And marvel how unwearied Nature dowers
With grace these alien wilds.   Blue as the sky
One gleams, all beauty: one of fiery dye,
Outflames the sunset, and the sight o'erpowers.
Others of lowlier aspect look demure:
Some calm as contemplation, or eve's star:
Others as infancy are bright and pure:
Many more brisk wear looks of Love or War:
Even like the race of men the many are
Vain, grave and dull, conspicuous or obscure.

SORROW AND SOLACE.

Written on receiving in Australia intelligence of our mother's death.

Our dawn, our pleasant morning light,—
    The noontide beam which cheered us on:
The splendour precious in our sight
    Is from this earth for ever gone.
No more in even balance weighed,
    Our morning and our noon are blessed:
Bright beams which from our zenith fade
    Have added glory to the west.

Hence fable deem it never more,
    That first the soul from heaven descends:
We have had being heretofore;
    Past life, which to this world extends.
By Plato taught this truth divine,
    And her whose soul has passed away;
Though pained no longer I repine
    That her dear form must now decay.

With God for ages had she dwelt:
    Had heard the words of Christ sublime:
Had all an angel's goodness felt,
    Ere she became a child of time:

Or never in this earthly sphere
    Such might of virtue had she shown:
A truth, a tenderness so dear,
    But from that Land of Love alone.

Tears did I shed, sad tears, not few;
    To think of days for ever fled;
As Death arrayed them in review,
    And made them lovelier through the dead.
But solaced, raised, no more I weep:
    She mourns not, wherefore should we mourn?
Unseen she marks the course we keep,
    And waits serene our home return.

When these dim lights of being close,
    The gates of heaven are nigh at hand:
Her hands will fold us to repose,
    And wake us in that better land.
No more to falter in our course;
    No more to faint—no more to fall:
We shall behold our being's source,
    All that was lost recovered all.

June 21, 1841.

OUR MOTHER'S GRAVE.

STREW flowers upon the honoured grave
  Where our lamented mother lies,
But let no gloomy cypress wave
  Betwixt it and bright summer skies :
Let freshest verdure o'er it spread,
  Let purest light upon it fall ;
For these resembled most the dead,
  In life, in death beloved by all.

Keep thence memorial works away ;
  Obstruct not Time's ethereal grace :
The Seasons there will tribute pay
  And Nature sanctify the place.
In solemn autumn, gladsome spring,
  Mute things to her will reverence show :
And there the birds she loved will sing,
  And there her favourite flowers will grow.

The sun from out the amber west
  Will touch that spot with lingering rays ;
The moon upon her place of rest
  Will seem more tranquilly to gaze :
The wind, that through the welkin sings,
  Gently as dies a summer wave,
Will thither come, and fold its wings
  To downy slumbers on that grave.

Whate'er is in its nature fair,
　　Whate'er is in its spirit good,
Around diffused through earth or air,
　　Or undiscerned, or understood:
With whatsoe'er she loved to tend,
　　On which she living love bestowed,
Will flock to their departed friend,
　　And cheer and grace her last abode.

Let there no painful tears be shed:—
　　A cheerful faith was hers, is ours,
Of truth divine through all things spread;
　　Of love divine in simplest flowers:
Of goodness past all suns above,
　　Diffusing light and gladness far:
The boundless confidence of love:
　　And knowledge like a guiding star.

The " Life in Life " she made her own
　　By thought, and word and virtuous deed,
Lived not nor died with her alone,
　　But will through future years proceed:
Whilst what she was on us impressed,
　　Is more to us than wealth or fame,
Will more conduce to make us blest,
　　And cause us most to bless her name.

July 18, 1841.

TO A SMALL AUSTRALIAN FLOWER.

STAR of Hope, with Spring appearing;
    Prophet of bright coming days:
Wakener of benign emotions,
    Happy thoughts, and grateful praise.

Now mimosas, out profusely,
    Hang their wreaths of paly gold,
Thee, e'en like a sportive fairy,
    In my pathway I behold.

Lonely in this region, pondering
    On the distant and the dear,
With a smile of kindly welcome
    Me, a stranger, thou didst cheer.

And with each returning season
    Round my footsteps thou dost rise,
To remind me, that our Maker
    Is munificent as wise.

Goodness ever from Him growing,
    Solace midst the world's annoy:
Scattering endlessly before us
    Life, and love, and living joy.

Thou art native in this region—
   Here hast had thy birth and death,
Since God called thee, in Creation,
   Into beauty with a breath.

Centuries was thy presence cheering—
   Whilst thy praise was yet unheard—
To thy every-day companions,
   Savage man, and beast, and bird.

Now the white man's eyes regard thee
   With a higher, holier aim:
Comprehends thy worth and graces,
   Though he names thee by no name.

Well he reads thy gentle meanings,
   Full of thoughts, in blooms and buds;
Nor can be unknown, or nameless
   To dusk wanderers of these woods.

To the sun they may ally thee,
   Who art common as its light;
Or, for thy seraphic beauty,
   To some star that studs the night.

Sure the rudest human creature,
   With no kindliness to spare,
As his wandering eyes rest on thee,
   Must be conscious thou art fair.

Sure the sternest, thee beholding,
    Ere his eye shall from thee part,
Softened and subdued before thee,
    Will possess a kindlier heart.

Half the term of years, or longer,
    To which human life extends,
We were strangers—now faith stronger
    Binds us than most common friends.

This I feel, thou lowly creature!
    Thou hast served me many ways:
In some things hast been my teacher,
    And therefore I sing thy praise.

I am pleased, thy thankful mate,
    With the lore thou ever bringest;
And oft to myself translate,
    Thus, some serious truth thou singest—

" Whatsoe'er is pure and graceful,
    Unto joy allied, tho' lowly,
Serves the cause of highest natures,
    Is God's servant, and is holy."

Therefore tho' thou, of the many
    Held be as a noteless thing,
I will prize thee in thy station,
    And thy worth will boldly sing.

Long thy light was from me hidden—
Soon will be no longer seen—
By the solid globe divided,
As we heretofore have been.

Yet when oft the eye is vacant—
When the soul recedes afar—
I shall see, as now I see thee,
Beaming on me like a star.

When thro' years and forms that slumber,
Memory sinks, from deep to deep,
Waking, I shall bless thy beauty,
Or in pleasant fields of sleep.

1813.

A RETURNED EMIGRANT'S LYRIC.

With England vexed, in discontent
On board a British barque we went:
Whilst bird and flower, whilst field and grove,
Strove with us, though in vain they strove:
Some farthest coast would we explore;
Would make our home on some far shore,
And see our native land no more!

Old friends from youth familiar, vied
With books to chain us to their side:
Old habits, feelings strove—in vain;
We snapped asunder every chain:
From many a hallowed tie we broke:
We heard not when Experience spoke,
Resolved to wear some newer yoke. .

The land we quitted in disdain,
And grew conversant with the main:
Familiar grew with sea and sky
In all their dread sublimity:
Saw either hemisphere; and found,
When the globe half was voyaged round,
A clime in which our hopes were crowned.

From life's old dream did we awake,
To mark a new career and make:
In Australasian wilds to find
A life more free, a clime more kind:
Old creeds it seemed were now outworn:
Old custom was a thing forlorn;
In a new land all seemed new-born.

We pierced with joy primeval woods,
We tracked the streams, we skimmed the floods;
And could such pastime ever last,
From us what weary world were passed:
Adam's old curse of toil were done:
Care, like a cloud, would flee the sun;
And endless holiday be won.

Delicious pastoral scenes were seen
Where only wilderness had been;
With endless flocks and herds astir
On man their affluence to confer.
The plough, too, busy—ox and steer—
And, mid the forest's sleep austere,
The axe resounding far and near.

Whilst here and there small open space
Spread lawn-like with a natural grace
Sweeter than art: to cheer the sight:
Full day in the woods' dusky light.

And homesteads small, with labour cleared,
Isles of the sea of woods, appeared,
Unto some alien hearts endeared.

And we too toiled for homes, for rest,
Each in the way that pleased him best:
Nor time was there for soft regret,
There was no room for memory yet.
Thought was in action lost, we wrought,
And from new scenes new ardour caught,
And to more leisure put off thought.

Our cottage rose—fields one by one,
The axe laid open to the sun:
On us the clime's sweet influence fell;
The land's new nature pleased us well:
Corn round us waved—our garden smiled:
With novel sounds were we beguiled,
And sights which vivified the wild.

What would we have? our hopes were crowned—
We toiled, and home and food were found,
Abundance blessed us: yet with these
There came the uneasiness of ease.
With leisure came a restless mood:
The backward-looking mind would brood,
On that which marred our solitude.

The golden years of life arose,
And would themselves to us disclose;

11

Old times, old friends, themselves display,
In scenes and seasons far away.
Nor vainly: England on us grew;
Australia into shadow drew—
And life's best charm was ours anew!

Our land was good enough of old,
And had attractions manifold,
For greatest men: our British Tell*
Our Milton, Sidneys, loved it well.
Such would have thought, did they contemn
Such land, our Shakspeare's island-gem,
God for it would have punished them.

Home-land, though thee we lightly leave,
To thee at length we fondly cleave:
Drawn, England, by thy soul benign,
We come to blend aims, hopes with thine.
Despite the storms which o'er thee roll,
In thee thy wanderer's heart grows whole,—
Hearth, altar, temple of the soul!

* Hampden.

Note. On my return from Australia, many years ago, because I
did not in the then almost general bankruptcy of the colony, recommend emigration, a Scotch Colonial guide-book manufacturer let loose
upon me all his critical vengeance. The head and front of my of-
fending had two other counts: One of them, that I had the audacity,
there being no act of Parliament to the contrary, to decide for myself,
after four years colonial residence, which was most congenial with my

tastes and habits, an old and highly cultivated country and condition of society, or a new colony. The other count was, that I presumed to think myself a poet. Byron was assailed by the bloodhounds of Arthur's Seat, and it was my destiny to be bitten by their Natural Vestiges. I would say more—but restrain myself with this consciousness—that I could afford to suffer injustice and contumely at the hands of one Scotchman, when I owe so much to others—genial and intelligent—proved in a life-long intercourse.

ADDRESS TO SCOTLAND.

Prepare the ship, I'll take a trip,
  Brisk summer winds prevailing;
To Scotland, realm of old renown,
  It will be pleasant sailing.
The ship is trimm'd, the sea is skimm'd,
  With an ecstatic motion;
And I in fancy's barque am borne,
  Across the mental ocean.

Grey Albyn; do I see thee rise
  Where Ossian long has slumbered?
Land of brave chiefs and mighty bards!
  The greatest earth has numbered.
Land of the Wallace and the Bruce!
  The Tells of northern story;
A pilgrim from the farthest west*
  Comes kindled by thy glory.

* Written under the assumed character of an American.

From out his mighty forests old,
　From prairies wild and weary,
He comes to see thy mountains stern,
　Thou ancient regal aerie!
Past Altrive Lake his way to take
　In tributary sadness;
To pause where death has cast a gloom
　Upon her poet's gladness.

To gaze on grandeur—on decay—
　In Staffa and Iona;
To muse on Morven's woody heights,
　Where sang the bard of Cona;
Awhile to fare by saddest Ayr,
　Where freedom yet is weeping;
Where beauty mourns o'er mouldering Burns,—
　And love sad state is keeping.

Wherever Scott has made the spot
　Most famous, proud to ponder,
By fair Tweedale, by Katrine's lake,
　In pilgrim-guise I wander.
O, Scott! who knows and loves thee not,
　An alien is to feeling,
In palace-dome, in cottage home,
　In temple or in shieling.

O Scotland! realm of old renown,
　Thou land of later wonder,

Pilgrims shall come to hail thy light,
   Whom widest oceans sunder.
And they who see thee but in thought,
   With music in its motion,
Thy wealth of mind, on every wind,
   Shall bless them o'er the ocean.

I love to shape thy martial air
   When the foiled Roman found thee,
But dearer art thou to the soul
   With song's broad halo round thee.
Time-honoured line for song divine,
   Thy sons' inherent charter:
Land of the heath-flower and the pine
   The patriot and the martyr!

Blackwood's Mag.

PICTURES.

MORNING.

Night's drapery dark draws crimsoned in,
Fold after fold, then grey and thin.
Dim crowns of stars the mountains doff—
Thin fringèd mists recede far off.
Wide day-spring has divinest gush,
Pearl, topaz, blent with orient blush.
Trees from their tresses shake the night;
Their myriad leaves dance dewy-bright.
High in the dawn, there is a spark,
A mote of fire, a sun-tinged lark.
A stream goes uttering joyous words;
Whispering round bends, it chats o'er fords.
A youth a mountain climbs, and will
On its bold peak stand rapt and still.

EVENING.

Eve o'er a landscape saddens down,
A browner hue and yet more brown.
The clouds are warm with sunset light;
Crimson, then gold, then dusky white.

A pilgrim's journey ending harsh
In sedgy wailings of the marsh :
Whose waning moon, a fragment dim,
Hangs on the dark horizon's rim :
Where ocean-waves, a weltering host,
Heave wreck and corse high on the coast.
Whilst broods o'er either element
Sad sense of desperate struggles spent.
His way the wanderer cannot mark—
But stands perplexed, till all is dark.

THE JUST AND TRUE.

Let us be just, let us be true,
Nor fear for that which may ensue,
The rancorous tooth, the sland'rous **breath**,
The life belied, the worse than death.

Yet, ever let our faith be strong
That right will right itself from wrong,
As misted mirrors keep no stain,
And waters vexed run pure again.

Let us not use the lash, nor sting
To quit us of the meanest thing—
But walk the earth with kindness through,
And we shall have a triumph true.

With shoals in shallows we may strive,
Love's death and prosperous life survive;
Yet on through darkness let us steer—
Right onward till grey dawn burns clear.

Soul's peace! how like a summer tree,
With shine and shade, with breeze and bee;

Or haven-calm, from tempests won,
With anchorage sure of duties done.

Then turn not, look not vainly back—
To doubt or waver in our track
Were but to breathe unquiet breath—
Were but a life, part life, part death.

Then let us walk amid the light,
Where honest worth is truest might.
Why fear for that which may ensue?
Let us be just, let us be true.

1845.

SONNET TO LEISURE.

"———— retired Leisure
That in trim gardens takes his pleasure."

Child of well-ordered Time! these many years
  Thee have I sought, yet thee I have not found;
  And yet how much by thee was to be crowned,
Ere fate stepped in with the conclusive shears.
With industry and gold, thy old compeers,
  Thou still art absent, linked with judgment sound,
  Whilst I still hurry o'er the Muses' ground,
Owing to song increased, and old arrears.
And much I fear, O, ardently desired,
  Full leisure! I must die and find thee not,
Where in trim gardens thou art far retired,
  Breathing still air in some rare-cultured plot;
For without thee, though every Muse inspired,
  Maturing Leisure! I must be forgot.

1848.

LIFE UNSATISFYING.

ADDRESSED TO A YOUNG LADY.

So young, so lovely, so beloved!
  And yet do you complain
Of the deceitfulness of life,
  And deem existence vain?

And say, that back towards your youth
  Two years you would return;
Of faith betrayed, of painful truth,
  Some lesson to unlearn?

Is nothing real, nothing sure?
  On nought can you rely,
Save this, that you are in the world
  To suffer and to die?

The heart's sweet flowers profusely forth,
  Youth's treasures did you bring;
And did the promise of your life
  Prove treacherous as the Spring?

It might, it must; and millions more
  At tardy time who sigh,
With weariness of hollowness
  The same will testify.

I'm thankful for such discontent:
  In such despair I find
That nothing in the world was meant
  To satisfy the mind.

Those violets a minute past
  The sense delighted well,
With youth's deliciousness—but now
  They have an earthy smell.

I'm glad they are not always sweet;
  I would not have them stay:
I would not have the world stand still
  In a perpetual May!

What souls of love! what shapes of light!
  That on our paths attended,
Have, like the sweets of odorous flowers,
  Up from the earth ascended.

Lady! I murmur not that death
  Grows wealthy and life poor:
Nor that we haste to overtake
  The travellers gone before.

O, lady! evermore for me,
　In sunset and in dawn,
Is something growing into light,
　But much more is withdrawn.

Thus, of the pained and purified,
　Are intimations given,
That even in fading flowers I see
　The outer gates of Heaven!

Jerrold's Mag.

GIRL'S ADDRESS TO A FLOWER.

The sun awakes thee with his rosy light,
  And the sun cheers thee with his early rays;
He calls thy tender beauty from the night,
  To share the strength and glory of his days.

He smiles upon thee from the misty hills,
  With fervent love looks on thee from deep skies,
And what of dewy sweet his warmth distils
  Receives, repaying thee with lovelier dyes.

Thou art not proud that he does look on thee,—
  As thou didst know his greatness, thou art meek ;
And seem a pledge of thine humility,
  This dewy tear and tint upon thy cheek.

Thou livest not unto thyself alone ;
  Thou takest and thou givest, and art blest ;
Around to thankful life thy sweets are blown,—
  And I seem thankless, wakeful, or at rest.

Oh! might I raise me from the darkness up,
  From the soul's night, as thou dost from the sod,
And fill my heart with dewy thoughts, a cup
  Of incense, purely offered unto God!

SONG.

Thou art lovelier than the coming
   Of the fairest flowers of Spring,
When the wild bee wanders humming,
   Like a blessed fairy thing :
Thou art lovelier than the breaking
   Of orient-crimsoned morn,
When the gentlest winds are shaking
   The dew-drops from the thorn.

I have seen the wild flowers springing,
   In wood, and field, and glen,
Where a thousand birds were singing,
   And my thoughts were of thee then;
For there's nothing gladsome round me,
   Or beautiful to see,
Since thy beauty's spell has bound me,
   But is eloquent of thee.

REFRESHMENT AT A SPRING.

I WANDERED from the weary town—
    Deep in my mind pride's galling sting:
And sat me for refreshment down
    Beside a homely village spring.

And as I backward turned my sleeve,
    To scoop the water with my hand,
Did there in poorest dress perceive
    A cottage girl beside me stand.

Who gliding there by me unseen,
    Became aware of my intent;
And, rincing twice to make it clean,
    Did then her pitcher filled present.

No art, no teaching could convey
    Into that simple act such grace;
Nor high-born child could more display
    Benignity in soul and face.

Politeness of the genuine sort—
    A chaliced daisy's yet undried:
A courtesy not of the court,
    But sterling, by the heart supplied.

Pleased was I, and like pleasure gave,
To the fair genius of the well:
That thus by her more than the wave,
Refreshed, all darkness from me fell.

Two hours gone by I had to wait
On business at a lordly dome:
And had been taught, mid pomp and state,
How poor a soul had there its home.

I had been angered on that morn
By a hard soul obtusely blind;
And thence had turned away in scorn,
And darkest bitterness of mind.

Then hail! unto the meanest shed,
To which the poorest shelter owe;
Where native kindness is not dead,
And buried deep in pomp and show.

CHURCH RESTORATION DESECRATION.

O, COME and see this sacred spot,
  See this old church's sad undoing;
And what some heads considered not,
  The resurrection sad ensuing.

I can't make out where Mary lies,
  And I have made most close inspection :
I found some skulls and bones of thighs—
  I do not like such resurrection.

And that poor boy who died so soon,
  And left his broken-hearted mother :
And who before another moon
  Were closely laid beside each other.

And now their dust is carted forth—
  Their ashes dug and hacked and shattered,
As, save for dung, for nothing worth,
  They rudely o'er the fields are scattered.

Folk where their kindred are may ask—
  Fond mothers for lost children yearning;
And find it is a bootless task,
  Homewards with saddened hearts returning.

12—2

What's of the charnel-house become?
   For once our ashes were respected:
And there as to a sacred home,
   Men's bones were piously collected.

Large funeral groups, I see them stand:
   The coffin'd dead, and friends who love them:
I hear the solemn service grand,
   That seems to open heaven above them.

A heavenly ray falls on the sward,
   With summer's warmth the mourners cheering;
But, with this reckless disregard,
   All grandeur thence seems disappearing.

That makes *this* seem unholy work—
   That, often in these cogitations,
I give myself a sudden jerk—
   And shudder off some queer sensations.

STAND OUT OF THE WAY, OLD TIME.

Written on seeing the dial in ruins in the *pleasure*-grounds of South-
well Union Workhouse.

STAND out of the way, old Time!
   With your scythe and weary wing:
You, in this poverty-palace
   No longer may reign as king.

Your symbol is shattered and rent;
   Its pillar crumbled and strown:
So pitch elsewhere your tent,
   And find you another throne.

They who have lost life's trial,
   By fortune beggared and shorn,
Care not for clock or dial,
   Nor whether 'tis even or morn.

O, were there good in the future—
   They here by the hour might watch:
Would hope come to the door-step—
   Or love lift up the latch.

They have had a visit from grief—
   Have strayed in error's den:
And find the cross and crown of thorns
   The bitter portion of men.

They care not for the morrow—
    They weary of to-day;
So break the dial that the hours
    May blindly ebb away.

Death is a visiting Justice,
    Who will not his hour neglect:
Of all inspectors the welcomest
    That come here to inspect.

Poor things! from life's dread battle
    Pursued by wind and wave—
They run unto death for safety,
    And anchor fast by the grave.

The few poor boards the parish affords
    To poverty that's a crime,
And a hurrying in of the mortal soil,
    And they have done with time.

THE LIFE CANOE.

Merrily, cheerily, down the stream
    Our life canoe sails on,
Till the pleasant wealth of youth and health
    All unperceived are gone.

And many a barque of tiny sail
    Is finally upset,
Where many a whirl and many a toss
    Amongst the rocks we get.

But broad, and broader grows the stream,
    The wrecks too many, though few;
As back we look to the haunts of youth,
    Dim in the distance blue.

Around the east the orange and rose
    Fade into common day,
As in our merry life canoe
    The laughter dies away.

And sweetest flowers, dear life canoe!
    The fairest flowers of Spring,
Fade round thee fast—around thee, blithe,
    The birds no longer sing:

The pleasant stream, the happy dream
    Of youth is left for ever;
And onward speeds our life canoe
    Down time's impetuous river.

Still broad, and broader grows the stream,
    And fast it flows, and free;
And now our human life canoe
    Is on the open sea.

Our human life, O God of Love!
    It is a sacred thing;
Over it spread, Almighty Dove!
    The shelter of thy wing.

Vast is the sea of human life,
    An ocean dread and dim;
And upwards from our life canoe
    Ascends a holy hymn.

O! need there is God's eye should mark,
    The eye unclosed by sleep,
Our course, now that the human soul
    Is on the dangerous deep.

His wonders in the deep we see,
    The agony, the strife,
And all the pleasant interchange
    Of various human life.

Gaunt death before us in his barque
 Is dimly seen to glide,
And life before his spectral prow
 Falls starlike to the tide.

Yet pleasant islands round are spread;
 On every hand we see
The isles of Love, the isles of Bliss,
 Gems in one human sea.

We touch on many a lovely strand,
 Through wondrous realms we pace,
Where God is seen in many a scene,
 In many a form and face.

We enter mighty cities—there
 On princely grandeur gaze;
And marvel at the skill of man—
 And his Creator praise.

And still we voyage,—voyage on—
 And seriously go we;
For many are the ways to Death
 Our eyes can never see.

'Tis a mysterious thing, O God!
 This life's precarious spark
Should cross the dread abyss of years
 In such a fragile barque.

This atom life, this grain of sand!
 That would as nothing be,
Against His anger, in His hand,
 Who framed time's wondrous sea.

Still on we voyage,—voyage on—
 Through storm and shine we go:
With the gales of death around, above—
 And the rocks of death below.

Sweet music greets us: whence that strain?
 From mermaid of the rock?
Or from some shepherd of the hills,
 Piping to his flock?

O music!—thou should'st not be heard,
 Thou soul of dulcet breath!
A sound of mockery dost thou seem
 In such a world of death.

There comes a wail upon the gale,
 The cry of human ill;
And now the sound yet fainter comes—
 We listen—all is still.

The wrecks are here, the wrecks are there—
 There's never a passing wave
But unto us the hillock seems,
 That marks a human grave.

Where are our youthful voyagers?—
　I marvel where they be!
The *many* that were, the *few* that are—
　How silent grows the sea!

Still on we sail before the gale—
　The unknown to explore:
Knowing our voyage is but *one*—
　That we return no more.

Hour after hour a slumbrous power
　Has wildly clothed the west;
The winds have died away—the waves
　Have rippled into rest.

The dreamy monsters of the deep
　No longer round us play;
The sun is gone, the stars are wan—
　The mist is still and gray.

How beautiful is youth—how brief!
　Unlovely is the grave;
Alas! our lifeless life canoe
　Rocks oarless on the wave!

Our sheltering ark through tempests stark,
　Our palace—home of pride!
And must we leave thee, life canoe!
　To perish on the tide?

A leaf upon a stagnant lake—
A reed upon the shore—
We touch upon the land of Death—
Our Indian voyage o'er.

THE RUINED HUMAN DWELLING.

I sought this spot in boyhood's bloom,
　This ruined human dwelling;
When in my breast there was no gloom
　Man's brightest hopes repelling;
I thought of knights and knightly worth,
　Through every country speeding,
No wrong left unredressed on earth,
　No human bosom bleeding.
I then would know of nothing sad,
　Do nothing that was vicious;
The sense of life, the bounding pulse—
　The feeling was delicious.
To me did our poor life appear,
A sun-like march, a bright career—
　In godlike deeds excelling:
A moon, a sun, were love and truth—
In the omnipotence of youth
　I trod this ruined dwelling:

Here too I came in manhood's prime,
　A fair foot with me paced it;
And in our bosoms was a clime,
　All brightness that embraced it.

Bright though it shone, from orient skies
   Sweet light to us beholden:
For love shed on it from our eyes
   A lustre far more golden.
We talked of lovers here immured,
   Of knightly lances shivered,
Of beauty long here suffering wrong
   By valour hence delivered.
How soft her hand in mine—her step
   How like a young roe's bounding:
A palace seemed this ruin old,
   The region, heaven surrounding.
The past was by the present cheered,
   All brightened our to-morrows:
How very light to us appeared
   The darkest human sorrows!
Our life to come had amplest scope
   For tales of fancy's telling:
With what a world of love and hope
   We trod this ruined dwelling!
In the dark lapse of after days,
   Autumnal-time ensuing,
I marked where streamed youth's golden rays
   Through this sad human ruin.
With altered pace I trod the place,
   To my past life attending;
And unto me like mournful grace
   The light of song was lending.

The old grey walls of crumbling stone
  In common light seen only:
With brownest ivy overgrown—
  Sad court and terrace lonely.
How strange! in youth no echo sad
  Woke in those ruins hoary:
The very air and light were glad,
  Imbued with former glory.
Now all is dim and blank and cold—
  And truth, sad truth is telling,
'Twas youth lent grace to this old place,
  This ruined human dwelling.

Hood's Mag., 1845.

THE HERMIT OF DALE.

PART I.

In Derby once a baker dwelt,
  A shrewd, observant man,
Who well the best of fortune's flour
  Had sifted from the bran.

Who had such store of golden ore,
  Of silver and of brass,
That up and down, "Old Money Bags"
  His current name did pass.

His looks were sharp as Christmas air,
  His eye quick as the hawk,
That even when his lips were closed,
  His features seemed to talk.

And thus it fell, to buy and sell
  His being did engross,
As he the only heaven and hell
  Accounted gain and loss.

Old palmers who in Marie's name,
  Asked alms from door to door,
Just glancing at the baker's house,
  To linger there forebore.

To linger there forebore, because
  As plain as house could speak,
It said fair Charity was dead,
  There dead and buried eke.

Moreover in the baker's heart
  There lived, and on his tongue,
Hard words for all the wandering race,
  Contempt, and bitter wrong.

Dark was his house ; a dusty gloom
  About it ever hung ;
Whence fell a deep mysterious awe
  On strangers old and young.

It was the spider's hall, the bat
  There loved to shun the light ;
Ah, me ! it was a doleful place
  For home of living wight.

The baker was a bachelor ;
  His love died in her spring ;
And thence through all his weary life
  He loved no living thing.

He loved no living thing ; his heart
  Was hollow, dead, and cold ;
As was the heart of her he loved
  Deep in the churchyard mould :
And thence he strove its hollowness   .
  To fill with hungry gold.

It was not filled.　An angel came
　Unto him in his sleep ;
And then that man of iron frame,
　Did moan, and groan, and weep.

O, wherefore was the baker moved
　To moan, and groan, and weep ?
He knew his morning star of love
　Beamed on him in his sleep.

He knew that gleam of golden hair,
　Those eyes intensely bright ;
The air, the shape, that charmed his youth,
　Though robed in heavenly light.

Out from the heaven of love there came,
　Out from domestic joy,
A spirit fair, the baker's peace
　To torture and destroy.

All he had loved in early life
　Were with him in his sleep :
His parents, brothers, sisters all—
　Well might the miser weep !

Uprising from those blessed dreams,
　How drear his hearth and cold !
He felt his house become a hell,
　And cursed his hoarded gold.

He lost his rest, he loathed his food,
    He joyed not day nor night;
Sweet memories of his boyhood came
    Upon him like a blight.

Dry grew his eyes, and hot: no more
    Sweet tears refreshing ran;
He moved about the house, or stood—
    A melancholy man.

Unto the Virgin-mother, then
    Unused to pray, he prayed
In agony of mind, that she
    His life would end or aid.

PART II.

O strange, O strange! O wondrous change!
    The baker's robes are fine;
His house is filled with pleasant light,
    He quaffs the rosy wine.

And can it be that doleful place,
    The miser's drear abode?
With gleeful guest, with merry jest,
    The house is overflowed.

All they who pass along the street,
    Perplexed sorely seem;
And rub their eyes, in wild surprise,
    As walking in a dream.

And can the music flow from thence,
    Midst gay robes fluttering light?
They see it is, it is the same—
    And gazing bless the sight.

All things of nice and rare device,
    Are by the baker bought;
Silver and gold with gems inlaid,
    By cunning workmen wrought.

Of each degree, the fair and free,
    Unto the baker come;
Of gracefulness and nobleness
    It is the joyous home.

With cates the board is richly stored,
    The board is crowned with flowers;
They laugh at pain; in purple rain
    The wine amongst them showers.

Ah, me! the baker's heart is sad;
    Amidst that noisy glee,
He strives his miseries to drown—
    A woeful man is he!

Whence throng these beggars all the street,
    Up to the baker's door?
The baker has a gentle heart,
    He feeds and clothes the poor.

He fills the hungry, soothes the sad,
    He makes the sick his care;
His fare is very good—his words
    Are better than his fare.

If pious deeds may aught bestead
    The melancholy mind,
The baker now should be at ease—
    His heart should solace find.

It is the midnight still—how still!
    The revellers are away;
And the Abbot of the Black Friars
    Is come with him to pray.

Is come with him to pray, for he
    Is sorely tossed in mind;
Nor in his hospitable mirth
    Can consolation find.

The abbot sees the iron chest,
    With locks, or six or seven,
And though his lips are moved in prayer,
    His thoughts are not in heaven.

Away the abbot bears with him
  A goodly abbey gift;
Yet no whit lighter is his heart:
  More gold than he could lift
Would scarcely seem to him to be
  Fit guerdon for that shrift.

And from the priory there comes,
  All smiles, like suit to press,
With sharpest talons, sheathed in fur,
  Like gentle leopardess—
And she bears back a gift with her—
  The Lady Prioress.

To rich and poor he opes the door
  Of the house which is his hell,
That happiness may enter in,
  That with him will not dwell.

Again there comes a change, O strange!
  That house is still and cold
As in those days of misery
  Wherein he hugged his gold.

The beggar sees it with a curse,
  Forgetting what he had;
And like an owl, the monk in his cowl,
  He sees it and is sad.
Never an eye that moves that way
  Beholding it, is glad.

Whither he's gone, there knows not one
  Of friends that were his foes;
And through the region round about
  The wonder grows and grows.

PART III.

O Deepdale! lovely is thy land,
  With pasturing herd and flock;
And lovely is thy hermitage
  Cut in the solid rock.

A cheerful place of healthful life—
  A spot of Nature's love;
With greenest grass up to the door,
  And crowned with trees above.

With that one arch before thee set—
  That one old abbey window fair;
The only wreck of the rich fane
  That restless Time would spare.

Hither, when Hermitage was none,
  The Derby baker came,
Deep in these wild and tangled woods
  His lone abode to frame.

Here, in the hollow oak, he made
   His dwelling night and day,
Whilst he, with unrelenting hands,
   The hard rock cut away.

For him, thus occupied, to cheer,
   The flowers wore looks of love;
For him the nightingale sung sweet,
   The thrush, and amorous dove.

And, though unnoted, on his mind
   The changes of each passing hour,
With all sweet hues and harmonies,
   Had salutary power.

And much was missed, through cheerful toil,
   That long had weighed upon his frame;
And joy and health, as from a fount,
   Gushed from his cherished aim.

Nor was it till through labour long,
   Perfected was this fair recess,
He felt, of his unworldly life,
   The quiet weariness.

But by degrees whate'er he sees
   And hears, have power to please him less;
And deeper, heavier, on him grows, ,
   That quiet weariness.

For him who in the town had dwelt,
  In daily sound of passing feet,
The still intensity of woods
  Had an oppressive weight.

But, shaking off that heaviness,
  Ofttimes he sought the village near,
With cheerful sight of human life
  His moody mind to cheer.

Serlo de Grendon, where is he,
  The owner of this wide domain?
In Ockbrooke woods he comes to hunt,
  And with him comes a noble train.

The stag has crossed the Derwent river;
  Has also crossed the broader Trent;
And, worn with that most desperate chase,
  In Deepdale now is spent.

Old hermit, quick, put out your fire,
  Allow no white and dancing smoke
To rise for Lord de Grendon's eyes
  Above the forest oak.

Wroth is the noble hunter—rage
  Fiercely possesses him: he sees
That light blue wreath curl up to Heaven
  From out his forest trees.

" Audacious wretch!" the noble cries:
" The villain, whosoe'er he be,
Who thus presumptuously hath dared,
   Shall hang on the first tree!"

Tremble not, hermit, be thou calm
   Howe'er the angry lord may chafe:
The cross that stands before thy door
   He sees—and thou art safe.

He sees that other image fair,
   Poor dweller of the woodlands lone!
The Virgin, whom thy hands have carved
   Religiously in stone.

He sees, he pities thee, nor can
   Thy prayer to linger there gainsay;
And of his mill of Borrowash
   He grants thee tithe alway.

Now happier had the hermit been,
   Would but that evil spirit rest,
That vexed him there, that tries him here,
   With various arts unblest.

That spirit, him who hither sent,
   In likeness of the Virgin-mother,
Appearing to him in a dream,
   Was Satan, and no other.

For hither by a gracious vision
  The baker deemed he had been sent,
In fasting, and in prayer to pass
  His last days penitent.

Again the evil spirit toils
  To work the hermit more displeasure,
To make him doubt his stedfast faith,
  And loathe his too much leisure.

Again he in luxurious dreams
  Is with most dainty viands cheated;
With wine, with beauty, and with song,
  His fancy strongly heated;
All his late joyous banquetings
  Are o'er and o'er repeated.

Alas! poor hermit, to thy crust
  How sadly didst thou waken;
And from thy tasteless water turn
  To what thou hadst forsaken!

The hermit prayed, the hermit slept:
  And like a phœnix from his dust
Arose the pride of ages thence,
  Dale Abbey's dome august.

Uprose it, as by magic, fair,
  In this secluded valley, still

With gorgeous images of power
    The peasant's mind to fill.

One arch alone remains—fair wreck!
    Fit emanation from the soul
Of architectural grace, to show
    The grandeur of the whole.

But thou, old hermitage, art here—
    Outlasting long the abbey's glory!
Memento, graven in the rock
    To keep alive the hermit's story.

SONNET.

ON "PARADISE LOST," AND ITS AUTHOR.

In hall, and bower, and at the peasant's door,
   The song divine from age to age is read:
   It was the charm of generations dead:
Still, like a river, flows it evermore,
Flows strongly, on, to Time's unbounded shore.
   And still we quaff it at the fountain's head;
   And, caught up by the poet, firmly tread
On air, hell's pavement, and heaven's starry floor.
What, for such wealth of mind, can we repay,
   Which makes us happy seasons in all years?
Most bitter payment found he in his day,
   In his ungrateful country's taunts and jeers:
And ours is (are we framed of nobler clay?)
   Love, and deep reverence, extasies, and tears!

Fraser's Mag.

SONNET.

THE veil'd stars through the breezy darkness shine,
    Mild as the glow-worms at my feet. Now sing
    O nightingale! and make the heaven of spring
More heavenly! The night, the woods are thine;
The earth, the heavens attend thee; sleep, supine,
    Will start up at thy voice, a living thing;
    The May-bloom will grow sweeter; the breeze its
        wing
Hush; and the darkness take a shape divine.
Sing, poet-bird! and I, by fancy led,
    Among the leaves listening, good Pan shall see,
Listening to thine, his own brave ditties dead.
    All the wood-gods thy auditors shall be;
And in this woody temple lightly tread
    Lest they disturb its sanctity and thee.

SONNET.

Oh! were I spiritual as the wafting wind
  Which breathes its sighing music through the wood
  Sports with the dancing leaves, and crisps the flood,
Then would I glide away from cares which bind
Down into haunts that taint the healthful mind.
  And I would sport with many a bloom and bud,
  Happiest, the farthest from the neighbourhood,
And from the crimes and miseries of mankind.
  Then would I waft me to the cowslip's bell;
And to the wild-rose should my voyage be;
  Unto the lily, vestal of the dell;
Or daisy, the pet-child of poesy;
  Or be, beside some mossy forest-well,
Companion to the wood-anemone.

THE MYSTERY OF LIFE.

Mysterious oft it seems to me,
How I a being came to be.
Since through the myriad years gone by,
Suns rose and set, yet lived not I.

Streams flowed, birds sung—the earth, the sea,
Were in their motions fixed, or free;
Each part was portion of a whole—
Yet I was not a living soul.

Of countless millions that have been,
No record lives, nor trace is seen;
Yet earth is green, the heavens are blue,
As they with death had nought to do.

And now I live, and breathe, and move—
Life with its wondrous powers to prove;
Awake to knowledge of things past,
In life—a life not long to last.

All natures since the world began,
Are subject to the mind of man:
Knowledge in insect, flower, and stone—
I learn all natures but my own.

The undiscovered, undefined,
In regions of the heart and mind ;
Where wing of thought has never soared,
Realms by the poet unexplored.

Revolving these—to ear, heart, eye,
Mysterious seems it man should die ;
So like a God, in soul supreme,
Yet evanescent as a dream.

Days, years pass on, and I am not,—
Like myriads heretofore forgot ;
A speck of life, a mound of earth,
Extinct as I had never birth.

A leaf, now green, now dark, now sere,
A drop of dew, a human tear,
A wandering wind that moans, then sleeps,
A rain-drop in the boundless deeps.

Ages in light sweet flowers will blow
Above, whilst I am dust below ;
And joy and beauty hand in hand
Make Eden of the living land.

O God ! and wilt Thou never more,
This life, resumed, again restore ?
Can that which knows there is a God,
Again be nothing but a clod ?

14

Great Animator of this dust!
O breathe in me sublimer trust
Than that which, grovelling, sinks to steep
This ending life in endless sleep!

My bed in dust and deepest night
Thy word can fill with heavenly light;
And make the flowers about my grave
With a triumphant beauty wave.

Thy word can wake Heaven's bow, to span,
With radiant arch, the grave of man;
Can fill with promise bright the void—
The doubt, the dread, to be destroyed.

This flesh may crumble, and this bone
In dust on wildest winds be strewn,
But at thy call shall wing its way—
Death shall be life, and darkness day.

ANTEDILUVIAN SKETCHES.

I.

EVENING AND NIGHT.

A SOLILOQUY OF ABEL.

THE flowers are closing, and the few first stars
Are dimly twinkling in the deepening blue:
The dewy mist, that riseth from the river,
In crystal drops is beaded on the stems,
On the fresh leaves and on the tinted flowers.
Few of the songs which cheered the open day,
Few, yet more loud, the evening cheer and charm.
No more the elephant beneath the shade
Reposeth, where the shadowy palm was cool;
No more the lion in the thicket lies,
Retired from noontide heat; the pard no more
Is, where the fountain gushed beside him couched;
The eagle, too, hath left his mountain home,
And with the lion will he share the prey.
Surely the eventide hath power to wake,
With its calm might in all things energy;
That thus all powerful natures are abroad,
Deserted thus, the eyrie and the lair.

14—2

The light that is a wanderer now departs,
Following its giver through the glorious west;
Following the faded crimson of the clouds.
Awake, O nightingale! voice of the night!
The melody of darkness body forth
The songs of loneliness.   Now, mighty things
Of solemn mood are present; now, the earth
Is hushed to hear thy music; wake! awake!
Silence is sad until thy strain be heard.
Sing, that the river's song be lost in thine,
And sigh of leaves, wind-stirred.   Awake, that we
No more may deem we hear our beating hearts
Listening intense amid the night-fall's hush.
The night is now thine auditor,—the stars
Lamps in thy temple of immortal song.
Sing! till thou only seemest in the world,
Stilling all life—all life by thee entranced—
Binding all souls in bands of ecstasy!

Fair is the dome of heaven; the stars intense
Burn in the blue, the blue without a cloud:
Dark is the earth, the heavens are clearly dark,
And leaves and flowers seem darkling of one hue.
Yet, beautiful is night! and silence here
In the awed soul stirs music; whilst the stars
Lead the free thoughts to follow in their track,
Paths to the throne of God; till the full heart
Pours forth its wealth in worship unconfined!

II

THE CURSE OF BLOOD.

A SOLILOQUY OF CAIN.

"And Cain said unto the Lord, My punishment is greater than I can bear."—*Genesis.*

THE land to which I fled is not the land
Of hope foreshewn, an outcast am I there,
A wanderer thence, yet hopeless I return.
Had Abel risen against me in the field,
Had he prevailed as I, him had his God
Of guilt acquitted—favourite as he was
Of God and man—then over both had hung
For evermore the curtains of one rest.
Why unto me descended as a dowry·
All that Eve's weakness earned of dark and dread,
Inheritor of evil! and from these
Why was alone exempt the younger one?
All that was lavished on most innocent Eve,
Prime in creation, soft and winning grace,
With Adam's dignity of form and mind,
To Abel falling as an heritage!
Favoured in life—but favoured most with death.

First-born of earth, the type of earthly power—
Henceforth the type of guilt, with power twin-born!

Of the slain *brother, son* to the bereaved'.—
Their pangs alone reproach me! Years! O, years!
Ye stretch before me like a midnight cloud:
I walk in darkness, and death's shadow vast
Is on me from the dead.   No more—no more
Goes with me forth abroad into the earth
Awe of God's image—safeguard to the pure!
Armed did we seem to still the elements:
Charmed, that things savage quickly changed or fled;
I by the elements am buffetted:
Fear from me rests no longer on the brute;
The lion, in the jungle starting, glares
Fiercely upon me with his fiery eyes,
Crouches, and scowls, or sullen stalks away.
This mark, which God hath in my forehead set,
Prevents them that they do not unto me
As I did unto Abel, or, ere now,
Silence had been my sepulchre, and rest,
That where I gaze departeth from the clouds,
And from the twilight dieth where I walk,
Had been my portion surely, as my will.
Why murmured I—why asked I aid of God
To shield me from destroyers?   Evermore
To breathe in exile from the painless grave.

Blood is upon the leaves, and on the flowers:
I see it when I gaze upon the streams,
The purest from the mountains.   In the skies,

In soft and silvery clouds of summer eves,
Are pale and dying faces. In hard rocks
I trace in sharp and cruel lineaments,
Of death the agonies, or awful quiet.
The shadow at my side assumes his shape,—
More real now than he. The very breeze
Sighs forth his dying accents—faint and few.
Where shall I turn, where fly, where long abide?
I may not change, and wheresoe'er I look
Earth still presents the same sad aspect to me.

I cannot be alone. Where'er I speed
Remorse doth fill the solitude, 'tis thronged
With all the children of the world of pain.
Wearied with wakefulness, no more from sleep
Steals there oblivion on reality.
Pain hath made one my being. Awful shapes,
Immortal in their natures, haunt my dreams,
That oftentimes from sleep, for which I pined,
To start, is happiness.

From the wide world
Have joy and beauty shrunk into the grave,—
And Peace, a dove with brooding wings, is there.
Depended these on Abel, that they died?
Methought that God of his immortal essence
Immortally of these had given—but they
Upon man's life depend, and die with him.

If in the soul beauty alone has being,
And joy the mate of beauty, and when these
Within us cease, they also cease without,
How abject am I in this lifeless life.
All then was slain with Abel, and I left—
Left darkly desolate, barred out from death—
Dead to the quiet of the happy dead.

III.

MYSTERIES OF THE FIRST DEATH.

SETH.

Why call you the young cedar o'er his grave,
The tree of Abel?

EVE.

In memorial
Waving its graceful branches o'er his tomb!
Sawest thou not the hillock?

SETH.

Yes, I saw
The little mountain with the many flowers;
The river, and the rainbow in the spray;
The pleasant shadows falling from the boughs;
And in the song of birds there madness seemed
Above me, in the trees and in the sky.

EVE.

The place is pleasant, yet a painful place.

SETH.

Why is it painful, mother? Is he not
Quiet in death as is the perished flower?
Methought, as I lay by him on the sward,
'Twas very strange that he was thus, and there!
That he must pine to see the open day,
The warming sun; to feel the stirring breeze;
To breathe the odorous breath of newest flowers:
And then methought there was enough of life
About us, and above us in the earth,
To wake him from his sleep, that he might be
A man again, to move in life with us.

EVE.

Seth! cease to pain me. Abel is at rest.
The living feel—the dead have ceased—they sleep.

SETH.

And will he never wake?

EVE.

           He will, my child!
When wills his Maker—never more with us.

SETH.

Perhaps to live with those who come, all light:
Who wingless move through ether, as they will,
Free as the winds; as graceful and as fair

As fairest flowers, or as the sunset clouds.
And is not such existence beautiful?
And blessed as it seemeth beautiful?
Abel perhaps may never be as they—
So free—so fair.   And thus it surely is
That death is awful, and is strongly feared!
Is he not living now?

EVE.

                    I know not, boy!
Who made him knows—that is enough for us.

SETH.

I would know more.   And when the seraphs come
Shall I not ask, if he abide with them?
If he be free to range with them through heaven?
And if he be, why not to come to us,
With those who come?

EVE.

                    Fond boy! he cannot come—
The dead have no returning from the grave.
And little with us now is left to tempt
Ethereal visitors—shapes rarely seen,
Familiar once—vain were thy anxious quest.

SETH.

How do I love him whom I never saw!
Had I beheld him, could I love him more?
Was it not strange that God should let him die?

He was most gentle, sinned not, loved you well,
Was most beloved of God—and yet was slain.
Methinks that He who made us from the dust,
Could from the dead have raised him with more ease
Than make,—manly, and good, and beautiful—
In nothing wanting, save the life, to be
God's finished work :—and he is dust again !

EVE.

How daring art thou in thy thoughts and words!
God is in all things just, and merciful,
And as He wills is this.   Had Abel lived,
Now hadst thou not—his death, to thee was life;
Thou art our Abel, with another name
To pain us not.

SETH.

O ! mother, had he lived—
My sisters cannot climb the mountains with me;
They cannot with me climb the trees and rocks :—
With me they sport along the plains and woods—
And Enoch is too young.

EVE.

Lov'st thou not Cain ?
Ask him.

SETH.

Love, yes—he is my brother—but,
I do not love him as I love the dead !
His face is dark, his looks are wild and sad.

I cannot ask—never when he is near
Wish I for aught.   I feel as sad as he.

EVE.

Go, haste unto thy sisters—hence—away—
I, too, am sad, and now would be alone.

Note.—On reading the above sketches James Montgomery wrote thus:—" I congratulate you on the time you have spent in the Antediluvian World—having myself lived some time in ' The World before the Flood.' "

TO THE BEE.

Odorous reveller in clover,
Happy hummer, England over:
Blossom-kisser! wing thy way
Where the breeze keeps holiday:
Thou art like the poet, free;
All sweet flowers have sweets for thee,
Insect minstrel! blessed bee.

Sunburnt labourer, brisk and brown,
Everywhere o'er dale and down:
Spring's blithe pursuivant, and page;
Hermit holy, Druid sage:
Pattering in a fox-glove bell;
Cloistered snug as in a cell;—
Fairy of the lonely dell.

Sometimes a small spot of shade
By the dappling maple made
Do I think thee, and thy note
Hum of cities heard remote:

Here and there, now more, now less
Seems thy droning to express
Noontide lazy weariness.

What sweet traffic dost thou drive—
Endless nature is thy hive!
Pasture after pasture roam—
Vagrant! everywhere at home!
We but see thy gorgeous bowers,
Whilst thou spendest all thy hours,
In the very heart of flowers.

Freshest feeling hast thou wrought
In me, of old homebred thought:
Of dear homesteads flower-o'ergrown,
Well in blessed boyhood known!
In thy warm familiar sound
Years of summer youth are found,
Sabbath, sunshine, without bound!

Temples, nobler none, are thine,
Where each flower thou mak'st a shrine:
Nor may any pilgrim bow
More devotedly than thou:
Gate-like petals open-blown,
Wide for thee, and thee alone,
Where thou com'st as to a throne.

Ah! how sleepy—thou I ween
In the poppies' bloom hast been;
Or art drunken with the wine
Of flushed rose or eglantine:
Boundless revel dost thou keep
Till o'ercome with golden sleep—
Tiny Bacchus, drinking deep.

Cheery pilgrim, sportive fay!
Sing and wing thy life away!
Never pang thy course attends,
Lack of love, nor feigning friends:
In a blossom thou art blest,
And canst sink to sweetest rest,
Homed where'er thou likest best.

SONNET.

SLEEP AND DEATH.

O SLEEP! delicious closer of sad eyes,
 Thou that dost make Care's heavy burden light;
 Sorrow's calm haven; that does clear the sight
To see fresh glory in the morning skies:
Did I not love thee I should be unwise;
  For when I start from thee in the still night,
  Thou watchest near me like an angel bright,
Divine, and endless in sweet mysteries.
 Death, were thy bed as pleasant, I would steep
My aching temples in thy slumbers, Death!
 In that thy rest is dreamless and more deep.
But then thou breathest not morn's odorous breath,
 Joyous, and oft-recurring—when from sleep
Lightly we rise—glad hours I fain would keep.

SONNET TO MARY HOWITT.

Oh, my loved sister! from the wise and good
  What wealth you gather of applauses rare,
  At Esher, breathing the delicious air
Of a song-memorable neighbourhood:
With books, with leisure, lane, and heath, and wood,
  With One, in all you prize the most, to share,
  Children at once intelligent and fair—
And by the world your worth, part understood!
  May song, which you have honoured, heap on you
Perpetual blessings: light that light procures,
The life of mind, the splendour which endures.
  More love you cannot have than is your due,
  More honour of the many, or the few:—
God prosper you in fortune! fame is yours!

1839.

FANCY.

My wings are light as gossamer—my way
Is with the sunbeam of the summer's day;
My pleasant car among the stars I drive.
And moonlight is the food whereon I thrive.
With a light sail I skim the azure deep,
The sea, the sky, and have a world in sleep.
Sometimes I clasp me in a girl's pure zone,
And feel all beauty like a flower full-blown,
Rest in her lap, or bask within her eyes,
As in the only real paradise.
The poet feels me kindling in his eye,
And in his brain, both which I glorify:
I make the poet's glance a glorious thing,
Which, like the primrose-footstep of the spring,
Leaves light where'er it rests.   But who can tell
My palace-home, the region where I dwell,
My airy habitation?   Is't where rise
Quick-spreading smiles round infant lips and eyes;
Or on the breezy forehead of the dawn,
Pale orange-tinted, dappled like the fawn:
Or is't where leaps and flashes the free stream,
Or in the rainbow's skiey-tinctured beam;

Or in the diamond dewdrop ?   Is it found
Still stretching on through space's blue profound,
Till, wearied with the vastness of the dome,
In a small flower I make my restful home ?
These do I visit glad, with frequent wing,
But dwell not in them, to them do not cling;
Mine is a temple anciently divine,
The heart of man, God's dwelling once, as mine,
Fairies my ministers—who to me bring
In dewy censers, all the sweets of spring;
Crown me with liquid brilliants from the thorn
And make me regal as the spicy morn.
I too sport round God's throne—but draw not near,
Awed by Imagination's eye severe—
Imagination, Wisdom's holy one—
Dark as the night, majestic as the sun,
Might dwells in her fair locks—her piercing eye
Sees at a glance whichever way I fly,—
Imagination's playful sister I.

SHE LOOKS UPON THE RING.

She looks upon the ring,
   In a dream of happiest days,
When the lips of one now dead and gone
   Were opened but to praise.
When life o'erflowed with promise
   Of happy, happy years,
In one dread day that passed away
   To torture and to tears.

She looks upon the ring,
   In the bloom of purest youth,
And can recal, remembering all
   His tenderness and truth.
The flowers he fondly gathered,
   And in her bosom laid,
Have never lost their summer bloom,—
   Those flowers will never fade.

She looks upon the ring,
   And the winter melts away,—
The very air is golden—
   It is the prime of May.

The fields through which they walked to church
　She sees—the bloom, the sky,—
And of the beauty of that day
　The sense can never die.

She looks upon the ring,
　And her cheek a moment glows,—
Again seem blending in her hair
　The lily and the rose.
She sees a bridal party—
　Of maiden white a gleam—
And the merry chime of village bells
　Is mingling with her dream.

She looks upon the ring,
　And her native home she sees,
As last she took a lingering look,
　Beyond the village trees.
She hears her father's blessing—
　She feels her mother's tears—
And in one moment knows again
　The bliss and woes of years.

NATURAL PRAISE.

High in the dawn the lark will sing,
    O'er mountain, and o'er river ;
Wafting that worship on free wing,
    To the all-bounteous Giver.

The thrush at eve, as sweet as loud,
    Of joy like large partaker,
Will sing amid the surging crowd,
    Yet louder to his Maker.

Wood unto wood, and stream to stream,
    In melody replying,
Till with the quiet of a dream,
    All sounds from earth are dying.

Nor will the nightingale forget,
    When darkness doth await her,
Sweetly to pay love's thankful debt
    To the adored Creator.

Whilst man, who cannot breathe in vain
    The breath of all things vernal,
Will, too, a joyful part sustain
    In song to the eternal.

SIMILES.

O! BOYHOOD is a mountain brook,
    That starts, and leaps, and curls, and foams,
That frets through many a flowery nook,
    To find a thousand homes.

Youth is a torrent, from the rocks
    That leaps, and shouts along the vales,
With glassy sheets, and stunning shocks
    That thunders and prevails.

And manhood is a powerful source,
    Of ampler depth, a graceful tide
Which in its daily gathering course
    Spreads health and plenty wide.

Old age—it is a tranquil pool,
    A haven of reflection clear;
A stilly place of shadows cool,
    And loneliness austere.

THE RAINBOW OF LIFE.

Hope, through youth's sweet April tears,
    Has the wondrous power to throw
O'er the fields of future years,
    Her many-coloured bow.

Only in the dewy time
    Of our being's morning march,
May we build, with joy sublime,
    Life's triumphal arch.

One by one the colours show
    In the landscape warm and wet,
Till complete the glory glow
    On the clouds' far-travelling jet.

River, rock, and tower, and plain,
    See, the gorgeous bow embrace;
Glorious pageant! look again,
    All is empty space.

The poet's eye delights
    Some inward vision fair,
The pen he seizes and he writes,
    Then looks—it is not there.

The heavenly bow his fancy made
　　Has left no trace behind;
Gone are the chords whereon was played
　　That music of the mind.

The painter, in some happy hour,
　　Sees in the earth and sky
Glimpses of glory and of power,
　　And holds them in his eye.

But when to give them lasting life
　　He toils from day to day,
He finds from that laborious strife
　　The glory pass away.

The graces of the morning hour
　　Fade into common light;
The sunset, with its gorgeous power,
　　Dies down into the night.

Alas! all beauty that has birth,
　　All splendour that is given,
To cheer, to glorify the earth,
　　Is but a gleam from Heaven.

SNOWDROPS.

A SONNET.

A LOVELY sisterhood of nuns ye seem,
 White-hooded, in your cloister of the snow;
 A sweet society, charmed to forego
Delights, whose Eden is the summer-beam,
Sports of the field, and hauntings of the stream.
 The lark will sing in heaven—the violet blow—
 The cuckoo shout—its star the primrose show,
When ye are fled, like music, or a dream,
 Sad am I for you, sweet ones! you must never
Wave your white beauty 'mid the summer bloom:
 In life, death's sanctity must you endeavour—
A sad content—irrevocable doom!
Nature has fixed your fate—*one cold for ever*
Winter your convent, and the snow your tomb.

Leigh Hunt's *London Journal.*

CHILDHOOD.

WE come to being from the night
As cometh forth the morning light;
The world is beautiful and new;
The earth is filled with flowers and dew;
Birds loudly sing on wing and spray,
And we—more merrily than they.

We gather strength, we run, we leap,
Find joy in everything, and sleep.
With mirth and beauty hand in hand
We take possession of the land:
Life surely *then* is not a breath—
What *then* has life to do with death?

A mother's love, her smiles, her tears,
Are with us in those blessed years;
The seeds of fond affection sown
In youth, that strong in age are grown:
Love that in part her love repays,
Her solace in declining days:

Light, warmth in age's wintry gloom;
Fair stars, sweet blossoms to the tomb.
Then knowledge comes with manhood's noon,
With care and sorrow, all too soon:
The springs of mystery are unsealed;
All that was hidden is revealed;
A common vision is the spring;
The rainbow is a common thing;
The morning and the sunset skies,
Are gazed on with familiar eyes;
The reign of wild delight is o'er—
And the bright earth is heaven no more!

AWAY WITH THEE, OLD YEAR.

THE pleasant, pleasant spring time,
　　The summer's gorgeous dyes;
The bright, the solemn autumn,
　　Have faded from all eyes.
I look upon thy features,
　　The furrowed and the sere,
Where lingers now no beauty,—
　　Away with thee, old year!

How wearily thou movest—
　　I would thy days were o'er—
For I have looked on some I loved—
　　To look on them no more.
Time's snows are on thy temples—
　　The desolate, the drear;
And a shadow on the future
　　Is cast from thee, old year.

So radiant was thy coming,
　　Thy promise all too fair:

But waned away from day to day
    To leave us nought but care.
Where are the bright, the buoyant,
    The beautiful, the dear?
Like blossoms of the spring-time,
    The prompt to disappear!

The dust of death has fallen,
    On locks of brightest gold;
And hearts of sunny temper
    Have changed to mortal cold.
The bloom, the bliss is over—
    The smile, the sigh, the tear:—
The lover is no lover,—
    Away with thee, old year!

SONNET.

THE REFORMATION.

To fields remote, through many a vale it wound,
  To grange and hamlet the glad tidings went;
  The shout of cities raised with one consent
To heaven: and smitten by that extatic sound
Rome's sceptre broken fell unto the ground;
  And cowl and sackcloth were asunder rent,
  Widely thro' British hearts was breathed content,
And cheerful faith, and thankfulness profound.
No more religion, hopeless as a nun,
  Vested in cerements of the sullen tomb,
Taught the pure air and face of heaven to shun,
  Was wedded to the cell's sepulchral gloom!
Joy flushed her veins, joy touched her cheeks with
    bloom
  All penances and monkish mummeries done.

SONNET.

ANDREW MARVELL.

In what fair temple of this famous land,
    Sacred to freedom and primeval truth,
    Whose honoured priesthood is perpetual youth;
Where, Andrew Marvell, does thy statue stand?
Genius, and love, and virtue, with firm hand,
    There wreathe a flowery glory for thy head;
    And at thy feet flowers of all seasons shed,
And circle thee with their immortal band.
Statue none hast thou; and unto what end
    Should local monument thy ashes grace,
Who better knew'st true honour to extend,
    Wider than statue, cenotaph, or vase,
Who wert thy country's and wast Milton's friend,
    And hast a place in hearts where these have place.

WITH CHRIST.

There is such life in all his words,
    As o'er from page to page we turn—
Such truth, such eloquence and power,
    Our hearts within us burn.
It cannot be the time is gone—
    We cannot think the era past,
Nor deem that in another clime
    And age our lot is cast.

As on we move from field to field,
    From village unto village on,
He, with the following multitude,
    Seems just before us gone.
We press to see whom thousands seek;
    We hear the glowing words they hear;—
Knowledge as boundless as the skies,
    And wisdom's language clear.

Him, when alone, we find alone
    Left in the desert place,
Whence his pervading eye and mind
    Speed through all time and space.
But how can he apart be left,
    Whom from man's haunts a space we find,
Who in his comprehensive heart,
    Clasps all of human kind?

" Entering the proud Jerusalem,
    We see him when he deigned to ride,
By an immeasurable stream
    Of people deified."
We think upon the health, the strength,
    The light, the life he gave;
We see him conquering the wind,
    And walking on the wave.

And in the dread and trying hour,
    When shameful death was near,
When the two spirits of the earth
    Were agony and fear;
When night came down upon the day,
    And death, as from a throne,
Seemed for a little space to rule
    The universe alone.

We see him bursting from the tomb,
    Whom mortals thought to slay,
Superior to the common bands
    Which fetter lifeless clay.
And in the sad, yet glorious time,
    Followed by mournful eyes,
We see him, till we see him not,
    Ascending through the skies.

THE STRANGE PREACHER.

" The man in the leather suit is come."—*George Fox's Journal.*

An old man there came to the market-place,
With a strong and a bold, yet a cheerful face;
And one after one people drew to the spot
Who lingered and lingered unknowing for what.

In the looks of the stranger, who stationed was there,
By the market-cross in the open air,
Was something they were not accustomed to see—
So they questioned each other of what it could be.

Some said 'twas his dress, which of leather was made:
Some spoke of his features' peculiar shade:
Whate'er it might be, the folks grew to a crowd,
And questions were getting impatient and loud.

With one word of his mouth they were silent as death:
When he stretched forth his hand was a pause in each
        breath;
And a feeling like thought through each bosom there ran,
That the being they heard might be more than a man.

In his words were such fervour, and fulness and grace,
And the truth of his heart lent such truth to his face,
Had he urged them to pluck down the town they had tried,
Although in the effort they vainly had died.

16—2

Had he spoken of wrongs which the people endured,
Of evils the people themselves should have cured:
Had he spoken of tyrants and tyrannous laws,
They had risen to shed their heart's blood in his cause.

But his words were of peace, and of truth, and of love,
And of One once on earth who came down from above;
Who, that peace might abound, in good-will to man,
Had endured all the pangs that humanity can.

Much spoke he of temples that were but of stone,
And priests clothed in purple whom Christ did not own,
Of merciless pastors whom Christ had foretold
Should seem to protect while they ravaged the fold.

Such a picture of Christ and his people he drew—
Of the chosen and simple, the faithful and few—
That, absorbed in the vision, they saw what he said,
And it seemed that his words gave new life to the dead.

They were chained by his spirit, they could not depart;
Conviction, like lightning, he flashed on the heart:
Though powerful his language, his aspect was mild,
And their thoughts were at once of a king and a child.

Ere he ceased all the strongholds of pride were o'erthrown,
And natures were softened though harder than stone;
When he ceased, in dim eyes were affectionate tears,
And in hearts a remembrance deep graven for years.

TO THE HOUSE MARTIN.

HOME art thou come to thy nest in my eaves,
With the flowery gems, and the light green leaves:
O'er the blooming earth, and the wide blue sea,
From a distant land unknown to me,
For the wise have sought, but in vain to tell
When winter is ours where thou goest to dwell.

Where the lonely ship sped on with the blast
Thou didst sink from thy weary flight on the mast;
When the storm had been, and the crew were lost,
On the shattered barque thou wert wildly tossed:
And didst float on the wreck, when the storm had died,
For days on the warm and waveless tide.

Where the lion crouched, with his half-shut eye,
In the jungle's shade from the burning sky,
Thou didst sit on the reeds o'er his fearful lair,
Pluming thy wings in the sultry air,
Till the negro's shout and his flying spear,
Aroused thee to instant flight and fear.

Still further on, still further on
Far as the mariner's barque hath gone,
O'er eastern seas he has noted thy flight,
And followed thy form with his wearied sight;
In vain—for no living wight may show,
When winter is ours where thou lovest to go.

Then come! and with thy return to my caves,
Dear is the thought which my soul receives;
If the mind of man, and his reason's light
Be powerless to measure thy venturous flight.
How vain is the wisdom which fain would find
The state of unbodied immortal mind:
Since little hath God unto man revealed,
And his future fate is a mystery sealed.

THE LAST SWALLOW.

Away—away—why dost thou linger here,
  When all thy fellows o'er the sea have passed :
Wert thou the earliest comer of the year,
  Loving our land, and so dost stay the last ?
Hear'st thou no warning in the autumnal blast ?
  And is the sound of growing streams unheard ?
Dost thou not see the woods are fading fast,
  Whilst the dull leaves by wailing winds are stirred ?
Haste—haste to other climes, thou solitary bird !

Thy coming was in lovelier skies—thy wing,
  Long wearied, rested in delightful bowers :
Thou camest when the living breath of spring
  Had filled the world with gladness and with flowers !
Skyward the carolling lark no longer towers :—
  Alone we hear the robin's pensive lay ;
And from the sky of beauty darkness lowers :
  Thy coming was with hope, but thou dost stay
  Midst melancholy thoughts that dwell upon decay !

Blessed are they who have before thee fled!
  Theirs have been all the pleasures of the prime;
Like those who die before their joys are dead,
    Leaving a lovely for a lovelier clime,
    Soaring to beautiful worlds on wings sublime:
Whilst thou dost mind of their doom severe,
    Who live to feel the winter of their time;
Who linger on, till not a friend is near—
Then fade into the grave—and go without a tear.

GIPSIES.

Now come in groups the gipsy tribes
  From northern hills, from southern plains;
And many a panniered ass is swinging
The child that to itself is singing
  Along the flowery lanes.

Stout men are loud in wrangling talk,
  Where older tongues are gruff and tame;
Keen maiden laughter rings aloft,
Whilst many an undervoice is soft
  From many a talking dame.

Their beaver hats are weather-stained—
  The one black plume is sadly gay:
Their squalid brats are slung behind
In cloaks, that flutter to the wind,
  Of scarlet, brown, and grey.

The slouching hat our hero wore,
  The crown wherewith he king was crowned;
Wherein a pipe and a crow's feather
Were stuck in fellowship together,
  Was by a hundred winters browned.

His sceptre was a stout oak sapling,
　Round which a snake well carved was
　　wreathed;
Cunning and strength that well bespoke;
Whilst from his frame as from an oak,
　" Deliberate valour breathed."

His footstool was the solid earth;
　His court spread out in pomp before him
The heath arrayed in summer's smiles:
His empire broad the British isles;
　His dome, the heavens arched o'er him.

Antique, and flowing was his dress;
　And from his temples, bold, and bare,
Fell back in many a dusky tress
As liberal as the wilderness,
　His ample growth of hair.

Like Cromwell's was his hardy front,
　Where power, but feeling none, was shown;
Where underneath a flitting grace,
Was firmly built up in his face
　A hardness as of stone.

From " The Gipsy King."

"These Gipsy characteristics have never been more accurately delineated than by Richard Howitt in his Gipsy King. The groups proceeding to the coronation of their king are living. The king himself is distinguished by some touches that are the life itself."—Rural Life of England, article " Gipsies."

SONNET.

IZAAK WALTON.

UNDER the honeysuckle hedge I see
  The meek old angler teaching his compeer,
  Making his art, with its nice mysteries, clear :
Meanwhile the April shower on bush and tree,
Patters with silvery footing pleasantly.
  Anon he tells him of the beggars near,
  Whom overheard he, and their jovial cheer ;
And of the master gipsy's knavery.
Happy old man! in his own temper blest;
And blest with noble friendships, many a one,
  Men chos'n from his whole age, the wisest, best ;
The lively Wotton and the zealous Donne :
  And they who gave his life its happiest zest
Herbert, and Hooker, Jewel, Sanderson.

SONNET.

THE SELF-CONQUERING KING.

Thou hast done nobly, thou hast bravely fought !
 Oh ! not for kingly state, or lawless sway ;
  At freedom's shrine didst thou thy sceptre lay !
And henceforth is thine empire in the thought
 And feelings of the free.   Power may devise
 A throne whose incense is the million's sighs ;
But thou hast won for thee a nobler state,—
 A more enduring throne : for worthless things
 Are crowns, and sceptres, and the sway of kings,
Compared with the high feelings which await
The givers of the gift of liberty !
 Hence is it that for thee the homage springs
Of all the great and wise ; and hence for thee
Breathes through all climes a noble memory.

Note.—This sonnet was applied by my brother to Alfred the Great,
I think very judiciously.—See article *Winchester* "*Visits to Remarkable Places.*"

THE NEW MOTHER.

THE STORY OF A LITTLE GIRL.

You ask me why I look so sad,
 And why the roses on my face,
Which ever bloomed so fresh and fair,
 Have lost their former grace.

And why I now seem so forlorn,
 Who was so very much caressed;
And wonder I who was so neat
 Am now so meanly dressed.

Long—long ago, mamma was ill—
 And when I went unto her bed,
When she had kissed, she spoke to me,
 But whispered all she said.

And when I went to see her last
 I could not wake her as she slept:
Papa sat by her on the bed
 And hid his face and wept.

Then many days to grandmamma's
I went; and often wished, in vain,
The clock and crickets were so loud,
I might go home again.

And when I with the kitten played,
My grandmamma would frown, and say,
I was a very naughty child
At such a time to play.

Glad was I when she took me home!
I far before her hastened on,
And very quick I ran up stairs
To see mamma:—and she was gone.

And when I called about the house,
And could not find her anywhere,
They chid me—saying, she was gone,
But soon she would again be there.

I often wondered why she went—
Papa and I both loved her well!
And always when I asked papa,
He would reply—"He could not tell."

Long, very long, she staid away;
And when again she to us came,
The day the bells were ringing so,
I thought she could not be the same.

For, when she went, her cheeks were pale;
  And when she came, her cheeks were red;
And then she came all dressed in white—
  And yet it *was mamma*, they said.

And so it was—and I was glad :—
  And loved her well, as I was bid;
Yet I am sure that she is changed—
  She does not love me as she did.

Note.—This little girl's plea for motherless children, when published more than thirty years ago, it was said, would cause pain in very many families. Surely one little sufferer may be permitted to speak for the many, that Christian duty may take the place, and remedy in part the loss of, maternal tenderness and affection. Good stepmothers,—and many such there are,
  "Their *peace* has no offence betrayed."

SONNET.

THAT many round me pour their living light
  I marvel not, nor mourn; much rather I
Would in their splendour lose me, than that night
  Should by the darkness shew me in the sky.
The roses red blush not with angry pride,
  Nor pine with sickly envy on the stem,
That snowy hawthorn blossoms at their side
  Obtain sweet notice—due no less to them.
The lowly daisy is a daisy still,
  Where blows the primrose or the cowslip fair;
Shewing God's gifts in as divine a skill,
  And by the same winds wafted, everywhere.
Blessed is he who knows how he is blest!
  With many sharing—bettered—though not best.

THE END.

www.ingramcontent.com/pod-product-compliance
Lightning Source LLC
Chambersburg PA
CBHW060614030726
47498CB00005B/1671